wendyl nissen's
supermarket companion
how to bring home good food

wendyl nissen's supermarket companion

how to bring home good food

First published in 2012
Copyright © Wendyl Nissen
www.wendylsgreengoddess.co.nz

All rights reserved. No part of this book may be reproduced or transmitted in any form or by any means, electronic or mechanical, including photocopying, recording or by any information storage and retrieval system without prior permission in writing from the publisher.

Wendyl's Green Goddess
PO Box 78-361
Grey Lynn
Auckland 1021
Phone: (64) 27 652 9800
Fax (64) 9 280 6450
Email: greengoddessnz@gmail.com

National Library of New Zealand Cataloguing-in-Publication Data

Nissen, Wendyl.
Wendyl Nissen's Supermarket Companion: how to bring home
good food / by Wendyl Nissen; illustrations by Alex Scott.
Includes bibliographical references and index.
ISBN 978-0-473-21442-5
1. Food additives—Identification. 2. Food additives—Code
numbers. 3. Food additives—Health aspects—New Zealand. 4.
Grocery shopping—New Zealand. 5. Cooking (Natural foods)
I. Title.
641.308—dc 23

Set in 11.5pt Mrs Eaves by Katy Yiakmis
Text and cover design by Katy Yiakmis

Cover painting and illustrations by Alex Scott
nzalexscott@gmail.com

Printed in China through Bookbuilders

Disclaimer
The information in this book is not professional medical or nutritional advice All care has been taken to ensure the accuracy of the information and every recipe has been personally tested by the author. However, the author and publisher cannot guarantee any material in this book in any individual case as reactions may vary from person to person. If you are in doubt about the suitability of any of these recommendations for yourself you should consult your general practitioner or a registered dietician.

contents

Introduction 6

1 Meat 24

2 Chips & Nibbles 56

3 Milk & Other Matters 78

4 Dips & Spreads 106

5 Breakfast 122

6 Bread 142

7 Meal Solutions 172

8 Cakes & Biscuits 196

9 Treats 220

10 Drinks 240

11 Sugar 258

Conclusion 274

Acknowledgements 285

Further Reading 287

Index 292

Food Codes 297

Food Eggs 317

introduction

why i eat this, not that

No one ever says, "Mmm, sodium stearoyl lactylate."

This is the catchline from an advertisement for bread. It shows a healthy woman with freckles on her face biting into a delicious looking brown bread sandwich filled with veges.

"At Nature's Pride, we don't think you should put anything in your mouth you can't pronounce. So taste the difference natural makes."

When I stumbled across this ad in a Martha Stewart magazine I felt that the advertisement summed up my attitude towards food.

One of my life's passions is to remind people about real food. The stuff my Nana used to eat, not the mass-produced, highly processed, and chemical-laden stuff that passes for food in the supermarkets we shop in today.

It started out as something of a hobby. I set myself a few rules to live by, which included not eating anything which had more than five ingredients listed on the label and not eating anything my Nana wouldn't recognise.

I got these rules from American journalist Michael Pollan, who has written extensively on the topic of the multi-national food-processing industry, "Big Food". He describes how, for the sake of profit, people are effectively being poisoned by the cheaper, mostly artificial substitutes for real food which are being incorporated not only into junk food, but food like frozen pizza, instant soups and breakfast cereals, which some of us regard as everyday food.

It was an interesting exercise for my family and me, and gradually our kitchen cupboards and pantry became stocked less with things which come in packets and more with things that get stored in jars, or sit on the kitchen table.

We made bread, yoghurt, cheese, jam and preserves in our kitchen. We ate only free-range pork and chicken, we grew our own organic vegetables and most importantly we ate free-range eggs from our home-raised hens out the back.

It was all going to plan and I enjoyed sharing the information I was discovering in my books, columns and radio work.

And then it all went horribly wrong.

I began analysing supermarket foods every week for a column in the *Weekend Herald*. I thought it would be an interesting thing to do, a chance to stretch the research skills I had learned long ago as a newspaper journalist. A bit of a challenge.

But instead, I just got angry. Angry that sitting on the very shelves which provide the majority of Kiwi families with all their nutrition were artificial colours banned in other countries, including the United States, which is generally considered to be rather easy on artificial foods. Artificial flavours which are hidden behind a New Zealand food standard which says, "It would neither be realistic to require, nor meaningful to consumers to be provided with, the chemical names of the individual flavouring substances present, even if they could all be identified." I found preservatives which had known health risks attached to them, unnecessary fillers like soy protein, used to "pad out" food because it's cheaper than putting real food in there. Artificial sweeteners which have turned up some nasty results in health studies.

And to top it all off — these things were only identified on the label by a three- or four-number code. A code no parent, child or grandparent could be expected to pick up, read and say: "Oh, that'll be sodium stearoyl lactylate."

Our food labelling laws claim to be a system by which every food product has its ingredients fully declared for all consumers to see. An open book. The information is there. Don't blame us if you make bad choices.

Yet no one has learned the language of *codex alimantarius*, which is the coding system used. And no one should be expected to. Why should we have to learn hundreds of different codes just so that we can make sure the food we feed our families is healthy and real? Apparently the code is necessary because many of the additive names are too long and complex for us to understand or for food manufacturers to put on the label. As consumers we are obviously too thick to deal with a word that has lots of letters that, when you put them all together, look a lot like a chemical name. More likely, some of us might be put off buying the food if we saw how many chemicals were in it. Much better if we just see a few, harmless numbers.

So I got angry. And then I got mad. With supermarkets.

I wrote a book called *Mother's Little Helper — an old-fashioned guide to raising your baby chemical-free*. In it I analysed a supermarket branded packet of baby wipes and found a chemical called iodopropynyl butylcarbamate (IPBC). My research found that it was nasty and certainly shouldn't be used on baby's faces. But then the *New Zealand Herald* got hold of the story and their journalist Martin Johnston found out that not only was it bad, it was really bad and banned under our cosmetics industry standards for use on children under three.

"Holy shit!" I said, when he rang to tell me his discovery. I also gave myself a kick up the arse for not having researched it thoroughly enough myself.

And within an hour of his phone call four brands of baby wipes were recalled from all supermarkets throughout New Zealand. Gone. Just like that.

I was very impressed and followed the story with interest, waiting to see what would happen to the people who produced these toxic wipes which had been used on our children for years without their parents having any idea of the harm they were doing.

But nothing happened. No fines, no bans, no

repercussions whatsoever for the four brands which knowingly broke an industry standard and were quite happy to charge parents money to rub the stuff on their children.

I swung into action, imagining myself as some sort of crusading journalist, to find out why. And I wondered, if these baby wipes were in the supermarkets undetected until I wrote my book, what the hell else was out there? And what checks and balances were there to protect us from this happening again?

In the end I didn't turn out to be a very good or confident crusading journalist, and so got some help from the then Green Party MP Sue Kedgley who agreed to write to the government on my behalf. She asked why there had been no action nor any measures put in place to prevent it happening again.

She received a reply from the then Minister for the Environment, Nick Smith, who said: "Due to the prompt voluntary withdrawal of the products and the co-operation shown by retailers, enforcement agencies decided that no further action was warranted."

He also confirmed that "there is currently no routine or random monitoring that specifically focuses on products targeted at babies or young children."

Do you see why I got mad?

The supermarkets were being patted on the back for doing such a great job of recalling toxic products that they shouldn't have allowed on their shelves in the first place.

Then I realised that two of the babywipes were Homebrand — made by Progressive Enterprises, part of the Woolworths family, which owns Countdown supermarkets. So not only was Progressive stocking dodgy baby wipes, it was actually making them.

And finally I realised that the products targeted at young children and babies referred to by the Minister for the Environment included food. Baby food, baby formula, snacks, biscuits. Some of the very stuff I was analysing for my column.

The lesson I had learned was that the supermarkets who present themselves to us as part of the family and who we trust to be the suppliers of all our food, have no reason, nor any legal requirement to check that anything they sell us complies with the standards (food and cosmetic) set in place to protect us. And the government is quite happy for them to be self-regulating as long as they get the shit off the shelves quickly when the same stuff hits the fan.

And that was it. Previously I had viewed processed food manufacturers as the Dr Evils of Big Food. But now they had an evil twin in the form of supermarkets who stocked the stuff and made a profit from it. Both were clipping the ticket on our health.

Then I did some more research on the structure of large corporations, such as Progressive, which is Australian-owned.

The truth is that if you're running a corporation, to quote Nobel Prize-winning economist Milton Friedman, "the only social responsibility of business is to make a profit".

Our supermarkets could be more careful and

monitor the products on their shelves to make sure they don't contain any banned and toxic substances. That would show us they are good people, putting their customers' health foremost. But any CEO knows that the costs associated with that sort of nonsense would undercut profits, and that's not what the business model is set up to do.

And self-regulation for corporates like supermarkets and Big Food producers is just ridiculous. As Joel Bakan says in his book *The Corporation*:

> *No one would seriously suggest that individuals should regulate themselves, that laws against murder, assault, and theft are unnecessary because people are socially responsible. Yet oddly, we are asked to believe that corporate persons — institutional psychopaths who lack any sense of moral conviction and who have the power and motivation to cause harm and devastation in the world — should be left free to govern themselves.*

I was so furious that I decided to boycott supermarkets and take my Nana life a little further back in time by only shopping at my local butcher, greengrocer and dairy.

"No one go to the supermarket," I announced at the dinner table that night. "We have to take a stand against this sort of corporate irresponsibility."

"How are we going to eat?" said Pearl, quite reasonably. In her 14 years she's never known any other way to buy food.

"We'll shop like they used to. At the butcher, the

baker and the greengrocer. We have all of those just up the road, right next to the supermarket less than five minutes' walk away, so it shouldn't be too much of a problem."

"But what about my stuff for school lunches? Snacks and things?"

It would be fair to say that preventing Pearl from going to the local supermarket would severely limit her style. She's a born shopper.

"You can occasionally pop into the dairy for those," I said confidentially.

Pearl didn't bother replying. She just looked at her father. This is what she does when her mother starts to behave in ways that make her unrecognisable.

"I know you've got your problems with the supermarkets but I think this might be a bit of an over-reaction," he said. "We already get our meat from the butcher and we already get our fruit and veges from the greengrocer, so that just leaves toilet paper. Are you planning to get that from the stationery shop?"

He had a point. We love our local butcher, who sources good quality free-range meat, makes amazing sausages and even makes his own bacon and prosciutto. We also prefer the prices and the local sourcing of our greengrocer, so had been shopping there for years also.

There were whole aisles in our local supermarket which we didn't go down anymore. We make our own cleaners and laundry powder, so that aisle is out. We don't do "meal solutions" so that one's out also, and we don't go near the meat or fruit and veges.

"Let's just give it a go," I said. "One week, that's all I'm asking."

And so the great supermarket-free experiment began.

I did baulk at paying $5 more for a packet of toilet paper at the dairy, and the only pet food available there was not only highly priced but something I wouldn't let near my pets. And as for the price of a block of cheese!

And then I realised that I actually had to go into a supermarket sometimes. I had forgotten that in order to write my *Weekend Herald* column I had to find a product to review. The only problem was that once I was in, it was all over. I found myself not only buying the review product but hastily stocking up on toilet paper, milk, cheese and petfood as if there was a war on or at least an expected natural disaster on the horizon. Not to mention shampoo and conditioner and my favourite tea bags.

"I know you went to the supermarket today," said Pearl when we were only three days into our experiment.

She had seen me while she was walking home from school.

"Can we just be like a normal family and shop in a supermarket again?" she pleaded.

And so we do, but where possible we go to New World or Pak'n'Save which are New Zealand-owned rather than Countdown. The least I can do if I'm going to support corporate greed which undermines the health of the people is to make it Kiwi corporate greed. And thanks to our supermarket-free attempt we do shop there less often than we did before.

WHILE I WAS writing this book, yet another story appeared in the news about what we should or shouldn't eat.

It was a list of 49 foods to avoid in order to prevent becoming fat. Among the many alternatives it suggested were a lot of artificial sweeteners, which I will never use. These articles pop up frequently and only serve to feed what I believe is intentional nutrition confusion.

There are many organisations contributing to this nutrition confusion. Governments with well-meaning bodies which release nutrition advice for the masses. Food industry lobby groups which "encourage" the government not to say things like "eat less meat", for instance, when every study you read says it is good for our health as well as the environment to eat less meat. And then there's Big Food with their nutriwashing. Making claims on their packaging of "All Natural" or "Smart Choice" or "Fat Free" when closer investigation reveals these statements just aren't true. And that when it comes to that word "natural" there is no regulation for what is required to make that claim. So any item, even if it is 100 per cent processed could call itself a "smart choice, all natural, fat free" product on their labelling.

As a result we consumers no longer have any idea what we should or shouldn't be eating on any given day.

I once eavesdropped on two women sitting behind me on a very small plane flying to Invercargill. They were discussing their diet, as so many women do these days.

"I'm just so confused about fat," said one woman. "One minute you're not allowed to eat it, so you eat something else. Then you're eating something else and they tell you that's bad for you. So you find something else and that's bad for you too," she complained to her friend.

"I just wish they'd give us all a pill and be done with it."

I found that conversation terribly depressing. I was looking forward to sampling some Bluff oysters and perhaps some blue cod in Invercargill, yet here was a woman who was so tired and sick of nutritional advice that she'd rather eat only pills.

Surely, one of the most wonderful things about being a living, breathing human being is sampling, tasting and consuming real, fresh, great smelling food. Yet as our food becomes more processed and artificial we are losing the ability humans were created with to taste when something is fresh, to smell when something is perfect, to see that something is beautiful and enticing. Instead we react like robots to packaging designs which issue instructions and deliver food which has been denuded, extruded and dyed.

One doctor who deals with overweight people in South Auckland was quoted in an article saying that the healthy eating messages were so conflicting and confusing to his patients that in the end he just told them to avoid food which was white and eat foods which were coloured.

Not a bad way to do it.

Nutrition confusion also feeds into people who align themselves with various food eating religions. Vegan, vegetarian, pescetarian (will eat fish), flexitarian (mostly vegetarian but sometimes not), lacto-vegetarian (does dairy but not eggs), ovo-vegetarian (no dairy but does eggs), raw food (nothing heated above 46°C), macrobiotic (unprocessed vegan foods, sometimes fish), paleolithic (what they ate 10,000 years ago).

I refer to these diets as religions because essentially they involve a belief system, whether it's avoiding cruelty to animals or believing that cavemen were healthier than us. It also requires a devotion to this belief system and the many rules and rituals which go with it.

In my social sphere I know of people who are anorexic, bulimic, compulsive eaters, picky eaters, overweight, underweight, you name it there's a condition for everyone.

In our own family we have two vegans, two pescetarians, two flexitarians (I'm one of them) and four meat eaters.

"I can't help thinking everyone was better off when my parents were kids and there was nothing to eat," I said to Paul one day as we had just finished planning yet another family dinner which involved three different dishes to satisfy everyone's dietary requirements.

My parents grew up during the Depression and

from the sound of it they ate bread smeared with dripping and not a lot else.

"It's almost like there's too much choice these days," I said.

Meanwhile, New Zealand ranks along with Australia and England as the top three countries in the world for "allergy incidents". Experts believe too many people are self-diagnosing and altering their diets, leaving out important food groups in the belief they suffer from various allergies without real evidence or informed help.

It is thought that 20 per cent of the population believe they have a problem but the numbers actually suffering from a food allergy are probably closer to between one and 2 per cent of adults, and 4 to 6 per cent of children.

In the UK, half a billion dollars was spent on "free-from" food, including ready-made meals, bakery goods, snacks and meat products in 2010.

There is no doubting that the extreme variety of things we can eat is doing us no good at all. For hundreds of thousands of years, humans could barely survive, scraping together enough food to get by. Our diet consisted of grains, vegetables and fruits with the occasional bit of meat, if you could catch it. Then we learnt how to grow our own food, and how to farm animals to feed us. That was how we lived for centuries. We didn't have problems like rising obesity and diabetes rates, which continue to soar despite the million-dollar weight loss industry helping out and governments releasing nutrition advice on a regular basis.

What we know is that in fewer than a hundred years the way we eat has changed dramatically — from the real foods my Nana ate before World War II to the vast array of processed foods we eat today.

In her book *Appetite for Profit*, Michele Simon likens the situation we find ourselves in to that of astronauts who have just landed on a planet with a mission to create a society where people get sick from eating the wrong food.

"First we would make all the least healthy foods cheap, readily available, and convenient to prepare and eat," she writes.

"Next we would concoct mysterious chemical ingredients in laboratories to ensure that the food is exceptionally tasty in ways that are irreproducible by mortal home chefs.

"Then we would market the hell out of these foods, in every form of media available."

She also suggests that the healthiest foods would be expensive and inaccessible and that cooking would be a lost art reserved only for highly trained professionals and television entertainment.

"Finally, our little band of interplanetary invaders would hijack the scientific process, suppress the truth about good nutrition, and deprive government programmes of adequate funding to promote healthy eating.

"This is exactly the situation we have today."

THIS BOOK STARTED with a suggestion from *Weekend Herald* readers who thought it might be nice to have all the newspaper columns in one book for easy access. It finished up being a story about a woman who started reading labels and what happened to her along the way.

I hope you find it mostly entertaining, at least informative and that in some way it might change a little or a lot about the way you eat and look after yourself and your family.

CHAPTER 1

meat

accept no substitutes

I have chicken bacon to thank for the fact that I write my food column in the *Weekend Herald*. That and the fact that my friend Deborah Pead had an "issue" with her mother, Anne, when she bought it.

"She was unpacking it from her shopping," Deborah told me, "and I said to her, 'Do you really believe that what you are holding in your hand is bacon?' She looked at me and said, 'Why wouldn't it be?'"

As Deborah, I and hopefully you know, bacon is something which comes from a pig. The definition of bacon is cured pork, not chicken.

During her conversation with her mother, Deborah took the packet off her and looked at the ingredients.

"It's only 72 per cent chicken. What else do you think you are eating?"

I'm not sure whether that chicken bacon was ever consumed, but I do know that Deborah and her mother continued the discussion in the car as they were driving north to the family farm. Both women are marketing experts, which is how it came about that Deborah gave me a call.

"Mum and I have come up with a column for you. We want you to look at things like chicken bacon every week and tell your readers what is really in these highly processed, mass-market supermarket foods," she said.

Actually she might have also said a few expletives when describing the highly processed, mass-market supermarket foods. She can get a little heated and passionate when she hits on an idea. She's also a very hard person to say "no" to.

"Well that does seem like a good idea," I hedged. "But a lot of work. And besides I'll have to get it placed in a newspaper somewhere, which won't be easy."

"Nonsense. You have good contacts. Just ring someone up, or take them to lunch or whatever it is you do to charm the pants off editors. And as for the work, think of it as good karma. You are changing the world."

"Karma, my arse," I thought to myself.

"Oh, and Mum has come up with a name for it. 'Wendyl Wants to Know'. That's the name, so make sure you use it."

And with that she rang off, instructions delivered and the presumption that I would get cracking and make it happen.

I have only myself to blame for this. Before suggesting this column Deborah also suggested I start my Wendyl's Green Goddess business and write the book *Mother's Little Helper*.

What can I say? She has good ideas.

I hung up feeling that if I tried to change the world any more than I was already, I might just out-karma myself back into bad karma. At the time I was writing three columns a week, plus my weekly email newsletter, plus finishing off my book *A Home Companion* and, with Paul, running a little business making all-natural cleaning products, the aforementioned Wendyl's Green Goddess. I was so keen to change the world that I even printed the recipes on the label to encourage people to make them at home, which my business friends found very anti-entrepreneurial. And the book I was writing was chock-full of natural and green alternatives to a life filled with chemicals and additives.

" 'Wendyl Wants to Know'," I muttered to myself as I plodded down the hall to consult Paul. "How ridiculous."

I was deeply aware that the blissful life I was writing about in *A Home Companion* had been out of my reach for some time. When I ditched my corporate career and moved back home to reassess my life, I tended my garden and hens, had time in my day to experiment with old-fashioned recipes for food and cleaning products I found in an increasingly large library of old books I had collected, and most importantly had time to exercise, or just sit and be with my family. Oh, and take off to my old caravan, which lives by the sea, for some "me" time. A caravan I hadn't seen for quite some time.

"I am not a machine," I blurted as I stormed into my husband's office at the end of the hall. He, like me, was writing a book also. He's a busy ghost writer who writes biographies for well-known people. But it doesn't stop me interrupting him whenever I feel like it.

"What?" he said, good natured as ever.

I explained to him the new column idea, how much I didn't need it and how much I wasn't going to do it.

"Sounds like a really good idea to me," he said. "And you'll love doing the research."

He was right about that. Part of my love of being a journalist is using the research skills involved, and my early training in newspapers in the 1980s made sure I was as thorough and accurate as I could be.

"What happened to my life?" I said storming out of his office and straight across to the fridge where I set about pouring myself a glass of wine.

"What's wrong with Mum?" I heard Pearl ask her father from the lounge where she was watching TV.

"Nothing. She's just been given a great idea for a column and is working her way through a few of the possibilities."

I glared at him.

"Why don't you see if you can get it placed and leave it up to fate?" he suggested, giving up his work and joining me at the kitchen table for a wine.

"If no one wants it then there's your decision made. If they do, then just get rid of one of your other columns. Like the Agony Aunt one, for instance."

"I love that column," I said sternly.

"Sure you do," he said pouring me another wine.

I let the chicken bacon idea sit with me for a few days, and then curiosity got the better of me, and I went to the supermarket and bought some.

"Look at this!" I said, to whoever was unfortunate enough to be in the kitchen while I was reading the ingredients.

"Crap!"

I then fried some up and tasted it.

"Tastes like crap!" I said to thin air as everyone had wisely left the room.

And then I sent off an email to a friend of mine, Shayne Currie, who at the time was deputy editor of the *New Zealand Herald* (he is now the editor).

"I'm emailing you with a brilliant idea," I started full of confidence. I might have also used the phrases "light-hearted and entertaining" and "ahead of its time". And then I finished with "I love it!"

This kind of confidence is not unusual for me once I decide to do something, which I obviously had. I owe my 12 years of working on the radio station NewstalkZB as a commentator and fill-in host to a similar enthusiasm for my own abilities.

"You should give me a show, I'd be fantastic," was apparently what I said to the boss at a function one night.

He gave me work, and I liked it, but I think "fantastic" might have been pushing it.

Usually when you hit an editor up to take a column, you don't hear from them for weeks. It usually takes editors that long to run it past management, consult the research, do the numbers, that sort of thing. And that's if they like it. If they don't, some of them just never get back to you.

My reply from Shayne came the next day.

"Great idea," he said. And so "Wendyl Wants to Know" began in the Saturday edition of the *New Zealand Herald*, the *Weekend Herald*.

Chicken bacon was, of course, the first product I analysed, and I don't mind admitting it took me two days of hard research. (It still takes much longer to research and write than any of my other work.) All the three- or four-digit codes used to represent additives on ingredients labels were completely new to me, and I had set a few rules for myself which were:

- I will only use sources readily available to any parent on the internet.
- I will not profess to be a specialist, i.e. a dietitian, nutritionist, scientist. I am just a mum going on the internet interpreting food codes for other mums and dads.
- I will only use sources that are reliable, i.e. not from some health group which claims everything gives us cancer, and not from an industry group which claims everything is good for us.
- I will support every finding with evidence. If I can't find the evidence I won't include it. (This was the most frustrating rule because I could have got some great headlines with the stuff people claim some additives do to us. Three-headed foetuses, anyone? It also takes a lot of time to find reliable evidence on the internet.)
- I will try to keep it readable, resist scientific jargon and, where possible, give healthy alternatives.

I FOUND THAT chicken bacon was basically chicken to which had been added artificial flavours, flavour enhancers, preservatives, thickeners, and fillers. I wrote:

> *After checking the ingredients, I have to ask: "Why does a bit of chicken need extra salt, sugar, protein, meaty flavour, thickeners to bind it together and phosphates to make it moist and tender?" Eating fresh reduces the need for all of these additives. My recommendation is if you want an easy chicken snack to make sandwiches buy a free-range chicken which is nearly half the price of $2.84 per 200g (even cheaper if you don't go free-range), roast it and keep it in your fridge for your family to snack on during the week. Ingredients? Chicken 100 per cent. Additives? Nil. And if you want to eat bacon, eat bacon.*

The column was immediately well received and both the *Herald* and I were very happy. But some people were not so happy.

I call them the Men Who Know More Than Me, and I usually get at least one email a week from their brotherhood.

"What you might like to know," is how they usually start before going on to spend an average of 500 (but once 3245) words telling me that I am a stupid woman with no idea what I am doing, and how I would be well advised to cease existing immediately.

It's hardly an exclusive club, as there seem to be an enormous number of them dotted around the country with their exceptional knowledge about anything from the chemical formula for salt to the nutritional value of a sponge. Most of them are retired from very important jobs with impressive titles which they still list under their name at the end of the letter but with the addition of (former) placed carefully in front of it. I hear regularly from (former) scientists, army personnel, accountants, engineers and one particularly persistent dentist.

"There are such recognisable, blatant flaws in what you write, why should anybody believe anything you write? Perhaps a bit more careful research and careful thought before you ride hobby horses," writes one.

"Recently (most likely because I have masochistic tendencies) I have been reading the nutritional articles you periodically write for the *New Zealand Herald*. This has caused me to ponder whether it is just me, or whether each and every article you write is a giant waste of half a page of the publication," writes another.

"Therefore, I can't help but think that, as a woman of pedestrian intelligence, you are laughing your way to the bank each week with the same disbelief as me that someone is actually paying you to Google the nutritional information on a single food item and format it under some bold headings.

"Finally, If you don't answer anything else today, answer me this, why on earth would your employers not give the task of writing this article to a proper nutritionist? If you say that is because it should be accessible to the average person, this doesn't work, because you have such little understanding of the topic that you have no ability to explain or simplify it (hence the half page of copy-paste jargon). If you say that it is because you will be able to make it entertaining, then this has failed, the article is about as bland as a Sizzler sausage," he continues (I've edited out most of the email).

Paul will find me frowning over my laptop as I decipher yet another letter telling me exactly how ignorant I am.

"Trouble in paradise?" he says.

"No, just another member of the Men Who Know More Than Me club," I say, scratching my head in an effort to work out what exactly they are accusing me of being ignorant of. I'm always more than happy to admit a mistake, and to date I've published four corrections (three typing mistakes, one genuine mistake) but these emails are never about facts, they are more about my impertinence at straying into their area of expertise (former).

"You know that you are making hundreds of older women very happy by occupying their retired husbands for the morning it takes to write you their emails," said Paul.

"Well I'm very glad to be of service, but you do have to wonder why they bother."

I don't reply to the Men Who Know More Than Me because it would just encourage them to write again and there's only so many times a woman can be told she is ignorant before she gets a little defensive.

Occasionally, Paul strays into my "Wendyl Wants to Know" email inbox, as he has all my accounts logged into his iPhone and sometimes enjoys keeping up with his wife's mail, especially over a glass of wine. I know he is reading my mail because inevitably he gasps. I count to 10 and then he gasps again. On the third gasp I've had enough.

"Are you reading my mail again?" I ask.

"Who on earth do these men think they are, and more importantly who do they think you are, talking to you like that? For old guys they lack manners and common decency."

I think for a moment about expounding on the certain existence of chauvinist pigs in the older male demographic of this country and then I just can't be bothered.

"Welcome to my world," is all I say, as I pour him another drink.

The other people who email me, quite rightly, are dieticians, nutritionists, doctors, food technicians and food scientists. They point out that they are experts in this field of food analysis and that they would be much better equipped to write the column. I agree with them all. They would. But the point of difference with my column is that it has to be easy to read and understand and written by another mum using the same tools they have on the internet. And while I accept that there could be some members of the food science industry who could limit their word count, use words people understand and do it all to a tight deadline, I've been trained as a writer for newspaper articles. I can relate to their belief that they are experts in their field. So am I. I'm an expert in my field as a journalist with 30 years under my belt.

My friend Paul Holmes, who broadcasts on NewstalkZB every Saturday morning, was one of my first fans. When I came on the show to do my usual slot at 11.15am, commenting on the media, he couldn't shut up.

"That column you are writing is wonderful. I love it. Everyone should read it," he said. "It's the best column the *Herald* has ever run!"

He has since started writing a column himself, which runs just a few pages behind me in the *Weekend Herald,* and would no doubt revise his opinion about which column was the best.

A few weeks later he raised a good point — again on air.

"You need to do a summary because not all of us have the time to read through all the ingredients. We just want to know if it's good or bad."

I suggested to my editor that we do just that, and now every column features a little highlights box for those in a hurry.

Processed Meats

After chicken bacon came Sizzlers (which are not really sausages), chicken nuggets, luncheon sausage, fish fingers, surimi, shaved lamb and canned chicken, which I have summarised at the end of this chapter for you.

There's something about processed meat which is just so handy. It comes to you wrapped up in plastic and sits in the fridge for ages until you need it and it tastes...well it tastes sort of like meat.

Most Kiwi kids have had a luncheon and tomato sauce sandwich and loved it. I have a friend who eats at some of the finest restaurants in town who loves nothing better than some luncheon and a bit of sauce even though I've sent him my analysis.

In some form humans have been eating processed meat for many centuries. The first processed meat was cured meat, preserved in brine or salt to stop it going off so that it could be eaten many months later. That is what bacon and ham used to be — although they bear little relation to the watery packets of slimy meat which passes for some bacon and ham at supermarkets today. If you don't believe me have a go at making it yourself (recipe below). The best examples of curing meat in my opinion are the Italian meats, like prosciutto.

Butchers have made sausages for many years and I can remember as a child going with Mum to the butcher and getting a free saveloy. I continued this tradition with my own kids at the supermarket, when they would get a free cocktail sausage from the woman behind the deli counter. I might be wrong but I would trust a butcher to make my sausages any day over some of the offerings I've found lined up in the supermarkets.

When supermarkets arrived, processed meats went into overdrive. They appealed to busy people because they kept for a long time in the fridge, were cheap to buy and fast to cook. But there's a reason for that. The reason is preservatives, which stop the sausages going off. And they're cheap because they contain fillings made out of meat byproducts.

Not a lot of real meat is in there.

The main things to look out for in any processed meat are:

- The percentage of meat in the product. Aim for the highest number because the more real meat in there, the fewer fillers.
- Sodium nitrite (250). You can't really avoid this in processed meat. It kills the bacteria which cause botulism and is a colour fixative, but there is concern that it can react with stomach acid to form carcinogenic N-nitroso compounds during digestion. A study has found that adults who consumed the highest amounts of nitrate and nitrite were almost 30 per cent more likely to develop bladder cancer than those who consumed the lowest amount of the compounds. Thankfully, some processed meat producers are now using alternatives, like sodium metabisulphite, which, when it comes to preservatives, is a better option, although it can be an issue for some people, including asthmatics, who have an intolerance to sulphites. (See Heller's Free Range Pork Sausage summary below.)
- Fillers. On the ingredients panel these can be hydrolysed vegetable protein, meat trimmings such as ears, skin and snouts, soy protein, semolina or breadcrumbs. If you're going to eat meat, eat meat.
- Flavours and flavour enhancers. These are usually artificial and are used in the product to help it taste like pork or chicken because there is so little of the real pork or chicken in there.

- MSG or monosodium glutamate (621). MSG is avoided by healthy eaters and it is accepted by the NZ Food Standards Authority that some people may experience symptoms such as burning sensations, numbness, chest pain, headache, nausea and asthma, but it says that it is okay to have in food as long as it is labelled. They advise people who have symptoms to avoid it where possible.

My Findings: Processed Meat and Seafood

Sizzlers

It takes 16 ingredients to make these and there are other sausages on the market with very similar ingredients. The problem for me is that more than half of each Sizzler is made up of filler such as soy protein, flour, water and additives.

Summary
- They look like sausages but don't have enough meat in them to deserve the name. The 45 per cent of meat is made up of leftovers including skin. People love to hazard a guess as to what part of the animal actually ends up in sausages, or Sizzlers in this case. Rumours of ears, lips and snouts abound and it is true that the tradition of making sausages came out of the need to use up all of an animal's carcass, which is a good

thing if you are at all interested in economy and honouring the death of an animal by bothering to eat all of it.
- A call to the Goodman Fielder consumer line confirmed that meat trimmings — what's left over when main cuts are boned and trimmed — are used in this product. All external parts of the animal are used, so that will be skin and, I presume, ears, etc, but internal parts, such as liver and heart are not used. If they were they would have to be clearly labelled in the ingredients list as offal.
- Sizzlers also contain sulphites and nitrites which some people like to avoid.

Hellers Free Farmed Country Pork Sausages

Finding a good sausage was once a very hard task indeed. Coming home from the supermarket with anything but a sausage sourced from pigs reared in crates, highly salted, full of preservatives and artificially flavoured was just a dream.

Now, thanks largely to the growing awareness of the inhumane treatment of pigs, major supermarket suppliers have started catering to consumers who reject cruelty, and like their food to be not "pork flavoured" but real pork.

Hellers is a major sausage manufacturer in New Zealand so I commend them for listening to their consumers and providing a product which we can be assured does not involve pigs being treated cruelly and which has such a high percentage of real meat. It also has no pork flavourings and uses herbs and yeast to give an extra flavour boost. Previously we had to go to local butchers to get products like this, so it is good to see them available in supermarkets at last.

SUMMARY
- Contains 84 per cent pork meat, more than many other sausages on the market.
- Uses herbs and yeast for flavouring instead of artificial "meat" flavourings.
- Uses vegetables rather than soy protein to fill the sausage out.

Tegel Crumbed Chicken Nuggets

At 29 ingredients this is a highly processed food item, and it has a few additives health activists steer clear of, such as MSG and annatto colouring.

SUMMARY
- Each chicken nugget has only 31 per cent chicken meat in it.
- Save yourself the 29 ingredients it takes to produce this highly processed food and serve your own chicken nibbles instead.
- Thankfully, most chicken nuggets in our supermarket freezers are made out of chicken breast meat rather than ground-up, reclaimed chicken carcasses and skin.

Hutton's Ham & Chicken Flavoured Luncheon Chub

When I'm feeding my children I prefer to avoid ingredients, such as MSG, sodium nitrite and carrageenan, which have negative health studies attached to them. I also like to give them real food, not something like this, which is only 43 per cent real, with the rest of the product being taken up by fillers, preservatives, flavourings and soy protein.

I also think we should teach our children what real chicken and real ham look and taste like, so why not cook up a chicken and keep it in the fridge? It only takes a moment to rip off some meat to put in a sandwich, and at $1.30 per 100g (if you buy a standard 1.3kg chicken) it is about the same price. Or buy sliced ham at the deli counter of your supermarket, making sure you order the ham which looks like it has come off a piece of meat, not been reconstituted into a circle. Good ham will still have some sodium nitrate in it, but you are reducing the amount of fillers and additives your child is consuming and giving them just one ingredient, called meat.

And if you really wanted them to have a ham- and chicken-flavoured sandwich, you could combine the chicken and the ham.

Summary
- Only 43 per cent of this chub is actually meat, the rest is fillers.
- Flavourings are added to make it taste like ham and chicken.

- Features MSG, sodium nitrite and carrageenan, which health activists like to avoid.

Fish Fingers — Independent Fisheries

There are 16 ingredients here for what is basically a bit of fish with some breadcrumbs on it. With any processed, crumbed food you are taking on extra additives to give it colour, keep the crumb mixture crisp and preserve the product in the freezer. You can make your own fish fingers, if you have time, to avoid unnecessary additives. Fresh hoki sells for about $18.99 a kilo, but you can also buy it frozen. Either way you are buying a fish from our waters which is managed ecologically and sustainably and you are giving your kids some fish in their diet, which is a healthy option.

SUMMARY
- Made out of hoki which is a sustainable fish thanks to industry quotas.
- Takes 16 ingredients for what is basically fish and breadcrumbs.
- Has the National Heart Foundation red tick and is high in omega-3 fatty acids.

Surimi Seafood Salad Mix

Surimi is a popular, highly processed substitute for crab meat which is made out of minced fish — well, half of it is, anyway. Possibly the least appealing use for it is when surimi is rolled into "crab" sticks, battered and then deep fried.

On its own it is popular with people trying to lose weight, as it is low fat and low calorie at about 1 calorie per gram of surimi. Most people are well aware it isn't real crab meat, despite the red "skin" used to make it look as though it has just been extracted from a crab shell. In fact, it takes 13 ingredients to approximate the real thing.

Surimi was first made in Japan hundreds of years ago but didn't become mass produced until the 1960s. It is estimated that 2 to 3 per cent of the world fish supply is used in the production of surimi, with the US and Japan being major producers and Thailand more recently becoming a big producer. This product comes frozen from Thailand and is then thawed for sale in our supermarkets.

I am very impressed to find that natural colours have been used to achieve the crab-like red skin on the surimi, even if one of them is obtained by squashing insects (carmine 120). And as far as I can ascertain, the Threadfin Bream fish used is not endangered by over fishing.

But I don't like the inclusion of sorbitol, which causes digestion problems. Some people only need to eat five grams to have a bad reaction, and I am one of them. I am also suspicious of the crab flavouring, which I think is most likely to be artificial as it is a cheaper solution to natural flavouring and this product is a low cost item at $10.95 per kilogram. If you really want to eat crab, then buy a little fresh or tinned crab and make it go further with low cost white fish, such as hoki, in your crab cakes or through a salad or pasta. The intense flavour of real crab goes a long way, so you don't need much to enjoy the taste.

SUMMARY
- Red colouring is natural.
- Uses sorbitol as a sweetener, which can cause gastric problems with some people.
- The fish used is not endangered by over fishing.

Kiwi Roast Lamb & Mint Shaved

If you take this product and look at it closely, there is nothing about it which resembles lamb as we know and love it. It is thin slices of something as round as a dog sausage, and it doesn't look or taste at all appetising. In fact it just tastes like something very salty and vaguely minty.

Yet I understand the appeal of grabbing one of these packs off the supermarket shelf and throwing them into lunches for the kids. So why not roast some lamb at the weekend, slice it up and keep it in an airtight container in the fridge and use that instead, if you really want lamb in their sandwiches. That way you are saving yourself 14 added ingredients. If you don't have time, at least pick something that doesn't contain an artificial flavour, like mint, or go to the deli counter and choose something which looks like it has actually been carved off a real slab of meat, not assembled from a congealed mass of meat trimmings.

Summary
- Not mint sauce, which we associate with roast lamb, but an artificial mint flavouring.
- Contains meat trimming, which can be skin and ears.
- Features cider vinegar, which is a natural preservative.

Chop Chop! Chicken Chunks — Smoked Flavour

When these little tins of canned chicken arrived on our supermarket shelves I found it hard to believe they would last long. Canned fish we were used to, but chicken breasts — which take a moment to cook at home — chopped up and put in a can and shipped in from Thailand just didn't seem right.

Yet, they have found a home in the hearts of Kiwis as the range has extended to 10 flavours and takes up a fair bit of shelf space, which means sales are strong. This may be down to the fact that bodybuilders just love them, though it's hard to believe there are enough serious body builders in the country to have that much impact. Chicken breast is low fat and a good source of protein, and canned chicken is a common topic of discussion on bodybuilders' websites. The commercial for this product claims it is high protein, low fat and has no preservatives — all of which is true.

You might want to buy locally produced chicken meat, cook up a breast or two and leave it covered in the fridge for two days to use in the same way you might use this canned chicken in salads, on sandwiches or crackers or with rice and pasta. This is also a little cheaper. For the equivalent 61g of breast meat, which is what you get from this can when drained, you will pay $1.70 for free range boneless and skinless breast or $1.22 for regular boneless and skinless breast. This product costs $2.14.

If you cook your own, you can take control over which meat you buy, free-range or otherwise, and know that you are supporting our local poultry industry. But, if you are a busy body builder and just want a quick shot of protein, this product does have the advantage of being light on additives and preservatives.

SUMMARY
- It takes seven ingredients to produce a bit of chopped-up chicken breast.
- Surprisingly low on preservatives, but does contain smoke flavouring.
- The chicken comes from Thailand, which has no animal welfare legislation.
- Properly cooked chicken meat does not carry nasty bacteria.

—my recipes—

Home-made Sausages

Sausages have always been a traditional way to use up left-over meat. In the old days the butcher would make them fresh at the end of each week and his customers would know to pop in on a Friday to get some for the weekend. There was little need for preservatives and the left-over meats were mostly fat and trimmings.

These days most people get their sausages from the supermarket, and by necessity they must stay in those fridges for some time without going off. So they have preservatives in them, and many have meat trimmings which can by law be anything on the carcass which isn't organ meats. That can include the likes of skin and ears.

It is easy to make your own sausages at home, if you leave out the bit where you have to squeeze all the meat into a casing. This is best done with a special machine, which not many of us want to include in our growing list of appliances.

So the best thing to do is roll them in breadcrumbs and bake them.

This recipe calls for some sausage meat, which I advise you get from a really good butcher. The stuff they sell as sausage meat in plastic casing in the supermarkets isn't great. Or if you are feeling adventurous, try making your own sausage meat from the recipe below.

By serving your family these wonderful Nana sausages you are stepping back in time to a day when sausages came preservative- and additive-free.

Pork and Thyme Sausages

    500g pork mince
    300g sausage meat
    1 small onion, finely chopped
    1 egg, beaten
    2 tsp fresh thyme, finely chopped
    2 cloves garlic, finely chopped
    3 tsp Worcestershire sauce
    2 tsp grain mustard
    2 tsp salt
    Sprinkle ground black pepper
    Breadcrumbs*

Combine the meat, onion, egg, thyme, garlic, Worcestershire sauce, mustard and salt and pepper. Roll into sausage shapes, then roll in breadcrumbs.

Heat oven to 180°C. Heat a little oil in a frypan, brown sausages all over then transfer to the oven. Bake for 15-20 minutes.

Time taken: 40 minutes.

*Look for Japanese panko crumbs in an Asian supplies store. They are crispier than ordinary breadcrumbs and better suited to baking.

Sausage Meat

Use this to replace the pork mince and sausage meat in the sausage recipe.

> 600g of pork shoulder
> 200g of pork fat (lard)

Chop up the pork shoulder into small pieces and place in your food processor with the lard. Process until it is well minced together.

Chicken Nuggets

> 500g chicken breasts or thighs (boned)
> salt and pepper
> 1 tbsp flour
> 2 eggs beaten
> 2 cups breadcrumbs or panko crumbs
> 2 tbsp finely grated parmesan cheese
> ¼ tsp paprika (optional).

Cut the chicken up into nugget-sized pieces and toss in a bag with some salt and pepper and the flour until well coated.

Beat the eggs and set aside in a bowl, then mix the breadcrumbs with the parmesan, paprika and more salt and pepper and set aside on a plate.

Dip the chicken pieces one by one in the egg, then in the crumb mixture, coating them well.

You can fry these in a little olive oil or place on a well-greased tray in a 200°C oven for 10 to 15 minutes, until they are crunchy and brown and the chicken is firm.

Time taken: 40 minutes.

Marinated Chicken Nibbles

500g chicken nibbles

Marinade

- 1 cup soy sauce
- 1 tsp chilli sauce
- 1 tsp finely chopped garlic
- 1 tbsp honey

Defrost the chicken nibbles if you need to and then mix all the ingredients together in the marinade. Pour over the nibbles and leave in the fridge for as long as you can (maximum 24 hours, minimum one hour).

Place in a roasting dish or similar and cook in a 180°C oven for 20 minutes or until sticky, juicy and cooked through. Serve with rice and salad.

Time taken: 30 minutes plus marinating time.

Home-made Bacon

This very old-fashioned way of making your own bacon is surprisingly easy and takes just four days. This bacon has just been salted, not dried or boiled, so it must be cooked before you eat it. My family loves the stuff. In my old 1845 recipe book *Modern Cookery for Private Families* by Eliza Acton, the instructions for this call for salt, saltpetre (potassium nitrate) and sugar. You can try adding a little sugar to this recipe if you want, but see if you like it this way first.

I prefer to use a herbed salt Paul makes, so I've included the recipe for that too.

And please use free-range pork if you can afford it. The taste is much better and you are supporting producers who don't raise their pigs in battery farms.

>   1 free range pork loin (you will often find it rolled and tied with string so cut it free and spread the loin out)
>   1 cup of sea salt (roughly) or herbed salt

Lay the pork flat and slit the fat on the top with several deep gashes. Take the salt and pat it all over the meat on all sides until it is well covered — we're talking about a 1 cm covering all over, so don't be shy and use more salt if necessary. Place it in a plastic container with an upturned saucer in the bottom so that the meat doesn't sit in the juice that will drain out of it. If you have a Tupperware container which has a grid in the bottom, this is perfect. Cover and place in the fridge. Check each day and drain any fluid which is sitting in the bottom. By day four it should be quite dry and ready to be sliced and fried, so wipe off any remaining salt and use. If you want, you can smoke it at this stage for an even tastier bacon.

Time taken: 5 minutes plus four days to cure.

Herbed Salt

>   4 heaped tbsp fresh rosemary
>   4 heaped tbsp fresh thyme
>   2 heaped tbsp fresh oregano or marjoram
>   12 peeled garlic cloves
>   500g sea salt or plain table salt (not iodised)

Finely chop the herbs and garlic. Mix with salt in a large bowl and let stand for 24 hours at room temperature to dry out. Place in an airtight container. You can use this salt to season pasta sauces or sprinkle on tomatoes on toast, but it is best sprinkled on steak before cooking and patted all over a chicken before roasting with a bit sprinkled inside.

Time taken: 30 minutes plus 24 hours sitting time.

How to Roast Meat

We roast a chicken every week just to keep in the fridge for sandwiches and snacks. You can do the same with beef or lamb and by doing so eliminate the need to bring processed meats with preservatives and additives into your diet. All these roasts can be stored in an airtight container in the fridge for a week. Leave whole and slice off the meat when you need it to prevent drying out.

Chicken

Buy a free-range chicken and rub some oil all over its skin then sprinkle with salt and pepper. Put a peeled onion, a lemon cut in half and any fresh herbs you have such as rosemary, thyme or parsley inside the chicken.

Place in a roasting pan in a 180°C oven and cook for an hour until it is crispy and smelling amazing. It is cooked when the drumstick pulls off easily from the carcass and when the juices run clear when a sharp knife is inserted into the breast.

Lamb

Get a leg of lamb and rub olive oil all over and sprinkle with salt and pepper. Get a sharp knife and cut little gashes all over the fatty side of the meat, leaving enough room to poke your finger in. Peel some garlic cloves and shove them into all the gashes you have made. If you've got fresh rosemary put a few sprigs of that in with the garlic as well. Place in a 180°C oven and cook for 15–20 minutes per 500g. Rest for 15 minutes before carving.

Beef

The best cut of beef to roast for sandwiches and snacking is scotch fillet. You need to brown all sides of the meat in a frying pan with a bit of olive oil. Then place in a roasting pan and put in a 220°C oven for five minutes before turning down to 200°C. A 750g scotch fillet will be cooked in 40 minutes. Leave to sit for 10 minutes before carving.

CONCLUSIONS
- Bacon is cured pork, not chicken.
- Look out for the percentage of meat in processed meats and aim for as high as you can find.
- Replace processed meats, such as luncheon and shaved meats, with roast chicken, lamb or beef, kept in the fridge.
- Make your own chicken nuggets, nibbles and fish fingers to avoid consuming fillers and additives.
- Hydrolysed vegetable protein and soy protein are used to fill in the gaps in food where meat should be.
- Make your own sausages to avoid eating meat trimmings like skin, ears and snouts.

Chapter Two

chips & nibbles

potato heads up

The first processed food I ever analysed was a packet of Roast Lamb and Mint flavoured potato chips. It was during a phase where their manufacturers were having a field day coming up with more and more flavour combinations for what was basically a bit of potato, oil and salt. "Roast Lamb and Mint" was already on the shelves but then arrived "Paua fritters with Lemon Wedges" and "Sunday Roast". I noticed when I was in the United States recently that they had flavours like "Dill and Pickle", "Fries and Gravy", and my personal favourite "Chilli and Chocolate".

Back home, I stared at the packets in the supermarket and wondered how many people buying them actually believed that through some magic of food science the chip makers took a meal of roast lamb or paua fritters and mixed it with potatoes to make chips. Did they mash it all together and then extrude it out into a chip? Of course not.

What they did was get some guys in lab coats to fiddle around with thousands of chemicals until they got a combination which, when placed on your tongue, made you think of the taste of paua or lamb. There are about 100,000 taste buds on your tongue, but when it comes to identifying a remembered food, like roast lamb, they are easily fooled. Which is really convenient for producers of mass market products like potato chips. Getting those guys in the lab to come up with the right powder to sprinkle on those chips is a whole lot cheaper than actually grinding up or drying out a whole lot of roast lamb.

That flavour industry is worth billions of dollars worldwide and justifiably so. With their chemicals the producers are managing to fool our tongues into believing that we are tasting a freshly picked, perfectly ripe summer strawberry or anything else they care to choose. It's food wizardry at its best and cheapest.

When I give public talks I hold up a bag of Roast Lamb and Mint chips and say, "There is no roast lamb and no mint in this bag. What is in here is some potatoes, some oil, some salt and a powder containing artificial flavour to make you think there is."

As I look out into the audience there is a sigh of disbelief which is so heart-felt that I can only conclude that the people genuinely believed that there was roast lamb and mint in the bag. Which is not a criticism of the intellect of the people who listen to my talks, but evidence of how much we believe when we read a package. If it says Roast Lamb and Mint, then it is.

As consumers we have not yet developed the

instinct for survival which has us passing the marketing information on the packet through a sieve of disbelief.

"It takes three ingredients to make a potato chip," I continue "Potatoes, oil and salt. How many ingredients do you think are in this bag of chips?" I say, holding up the Roast Lamb and Mint bag.

Silence.

"Twenty-seven."

This time the reaction is more shock than disbelief, and that's when people start shaking their heads vigorously from side to side, the universal sign for "You have got to be kidding me!"

"If it takes three ingredients to make potato chips, that means this product uses 24 ingredients which are essentially chemicals to make a potato chip taste like Roast Lamb and Mint."

Sometimes I throw in the word "massive" before the "24 ingredients" for effect.

What then happens is that my listeners start to look a bit unhappy and miserable as the knowledge dawns on them that they can't eat potato chips any more.

"Are these chemicals in all the chips we buy?" someone usually asks.

And that's when I hold up a packet of plain old potato chips, the kind that have been around forever. There is usually some red on the packet, for some reason.

"Don't worry. You can still eat chips," I say. "Just make sure you read the ingredients panel, like the one on this packet which says 'potatoes, oil, salt.' "

I know as a public speaker there are two rules for how you leave your audience. One is wanting more, the other is happy.

Potato chips satisfy the three primary food attributes we humans have come to love as we have evolved: fat, salt and carbohydrates. I have yet to meet a person who does not like the taste of a thin slice of potato deep fried and smothered in salt.

In our earliest years as humans, when food was hard to find, we evolved to seek out those that were high in salt, fat and carbohydrates because these were also the highest in nutrients and calories. And so your tastebuds will always have a primal celebration if you run these flavours over your tongue. They are rejoicing that in a body designed and prepared for famine for hundreds of thousands of years, you have managed to find some fat, salt and carbs. Well done, you.

But in just a few decades fatty, salty, carb-high foods which have been stripped of most of their nutrients by being processed and stored for months are available in abundance. And that's one reason why our new constant companions, obesity and diabetes, have become such scary diseases, affecting a growing and startling number of people around the world.

About once or twice a year Paul and I decide to throw a party. It's usually because one (or both) of us has been in semi-hibernation finishing a book and we're desperate for some social interaction with our friends, or just because we feel like having a party. Who needs an excuse?

Our last party was held mainly to consume the many litres of apple cider which we had put down the year before and was finally ready to drink. A bit of a tip here for anyone thinking of doing the same. Do not warn your guests as they walk through the door that you don't know how potent the cider is. They'll all be too scared to try it and you'll still have half the cider left at the end of the night. Not counting the couple of friends who didn't hear you or didn't care and had a very enjoyable night and a massive hangover the next day.

We had a few kids coming, so I put out bowls of plain potato chips — the ones with just three ingredients — and some hummus to keep them going until we served the main food.

I handed them around to the adults and saw a close friend pull back in horror when I put them under her nose.

"You eat those?" she said. "With everything you know from writing your column?"

"Yeah, these ones are fine, no additives," I reassured her.

She put her hands on her hips and glared at me.

"Ever since you analysed those Roast Lamb and Mint potato chips in the paper we have banned potato chips from our house. And now you're telling me that all this time we could have been eating these?"

"Why didn't you look at the ingredients?" I asked. My friend is a very intelligent woman and quite capable of analysing a label.

"Who has the time?" she replied as she grabbed

a handful of chips and went off happily crunching into the longed-for fatty, salty, carby motherlode.

Her husband was over in a jiffy.

"We haven't had potato chips for a year," he said, grabbing a handful with joy.

My friend's reaction is an illustration of how easy it is to frighten people in this world where we are bombarded with nutritional advice about foods we must eat, foods we must not eat, foods we can eat sometimes, foods some person who has lived to 123 years ate every day of their lives, foods which will prevent cancer, foods cavemen ate.

Making a simple decision about what to eat as a snack, let alone what to feed a family can be challenging, and it's no wonder so many of us give up after a hard week at work and dial for a pizza on a Friday night (then spend the rest of the weekend feeling guilty).

I believe that we were all better off in my Nana's day, which was the early 1900s, when there was much less choice about what to eat. Before the world discovered factories and mass production there were veges and fruit from the garden, or your preserves from the pantry, meat from the butcher, fish caught at the weekend, milk delivered fresh and unadulterated every morning, cheese, bread and baking. Oh, and some rice and sago.

ONE FOOD THEY would never have heard of, unless they were Mexican, is corn chips.

I first discovered these when I lived in the United States as an exchange student in 1979. I sent bags of them back home for my family to try, but their letters were strangely silent about this new taste sensation.

When I returned home they admitted that when they arrived they were all broken into tiny pieces and "smelled funny".

These days corn chips and tacos are staple offerings for Kiwi families. The good news is that corn chips are a lot like potato chips.

If you choose an unflavoured, regular pack — again, usually with red as its main colour — the ingredients list will tell you that all it contains is corn and vegetable oil. Not even salt.

If you start looking at flavoured corn chips, then that's when you start seeing additives such as artificial flavouring, preservatives, stuff to make the flavour stick on the chips and colourings.

But cheese flavouring isn't too bad, as I was pleased to find when I looked into my personal all-time favourite snack food, which I have been eating since I started school — Twisties.

Extruded corn snacks were invented in the 1930s, when a factory which was flaking corn to produce livestock feed discovered that if they moistened the mix it came out puffed up at the end of the process. The result was Twisties. These, therefore, are a highly processed food but they rate a little higher than other flavoured snacks because the cheese flavouring is sourced from milk solids, not chemicals. So as a general rule, if you're choosing a flavoured snack, the cheesier it is, the fewer chemicals you are getting.

Butter flavouring, in contrast, is not a great choice, as I discovered when I looked into some butter-flavoured popcorn. First, there was no butter in the ingredients list, and second there was no indication on the label as to what exactly was used to imitate the taste of butter.

My research found that in recent years the main ingredient of artificial butter flavour — diacetyl — was found to cause bronchiolitis obliterans, a rare and serious disease of the lungs, in factories where the flavouring was made. It became known as "Popcorn Worker's Lung" and lawsuits followed. But you can be relieved to know that in December 2007, ConAgra Foods, the makers of this popcorn, announced it had removed diacetyl from all of its butter-flavoured microwave popcorn.

ANOTHER SNACK I was asked to look into was seaweed, as I was told it was the new must-have addition to children's lunchboxes. Snack packs of seasoned seaweed are sold in most supermarkets and children seem to enjoy the spicy, fishy, salty, crunchy flavour. And not just kids. I loved them and had been consuming them for about a year, along with my son Daniel.

The snacks are strips of nori, which is the seaweed which surrounds sushi, cut into pieces and seasoned. Some mothers were worried that the seaweed was too salty, contained too much iodine and, if imported from Japan, might contain radionuclides, after the meltdown of nuclear power plants during the 2011 earthquake.

The good news is that seaweed is extremely nutritious, with a variety of minerals such as calcium, magnesium and potassium, it is low calorie and many people believe it is a superfood which boosts the immune system, reduces blood sugar and cholesterol levels and decreases the symptoms of arthritis.

This sort of seaweed (nori) has one of the lowest levels of iodine at 16 mcg/g but eating a 16g pack of this snack would give you 256mcg of iodine, which I realised was twice the recommended daily allowance for a child.

According to Food Standards Australia New Zealand, the recommended daily intake of iodine for adults is 150 mcg and children 90mcg (ages one to eight) to 120mcg (ages nine to 13). So you wouldn't want to be eating one pack of these a day, because too much iodine can lead to hyperthyroidism (overactive thyroid causing symptoms including palpitations, fatigue and weight loss) while low levels can cause hypothyroidism (underactive thyroid causing fatigue, weight gain and confusion). In New Zealand, we don't have iodine in our soil, which is why we are encouraged to eat iodised salt, and all bread must have iodine added to it.

By comparison kelp has 8165mcg/g and oysters have 60mcg/g.

A report in the Australian newspaper *The Age* said the Australian Federal Department of Health and Ageing was so alarmed by the increasing number of people with thyroid conditions linked to seaweed through sushi consumption that it issued a warning to doctors, endocrinologists and state and territory chief health officers last year.

As for radioactivity, Food Standards Australia and New Zealand said that the risk is "negligible".

Crackers and cheese are an age-old snack which my Nana ate on a regular basis. I can remember her setting out a plate of Huntley & Palmers water crackers, smeared with butter onto which a slice of cheddar had been placed. As long as your crackers aren't too high in fat or sugar and don't have any flavourings added, this is a great snack for kids and easy to prepare.

In my house this is our snack of choice, closely followed by homemade potato chips (recipe below) and fruit and nuts.

In general, however, when it comes to fruit as a snack choice, good luck getting your child to pick that option. It's a great idea in theory, but you're up against it when there are whole aisles in the supermarket, and million-dollar ad campaigns on the TV, designed to pull your child away into a world where their favourite cartoon character tells them to have something fatty, salty and carby out of a fun, colourful bag.

When was the last time you saw an advertisement for fruit aimed at your child?

And to be honest, I'm with the kids, because so much of the fruit you buy at the supermarkets tastes terrible. Floury apples which have been in storage for months, long past when they were picked fresh from the tree and full of nutrition. Or how about a dry old orange imported from the United States under some ridiculous trade agreement which denies us our own fruit from our own orchards. I use a lot of lemons in my cooking (and my gin and tonics) and until the four trees I have planted get their act together and start producing I am reliant on the supermarkets. How is it that in the middle of winter — when lemons are in season and abundant in backyards all over the country — the only lemons on offer locally have an "Origin: USA" label?

But put my grand-daughter Lila and me in front of our strawberry plant or under our plum tree when the fruit is just picked, and you'll have a hard time stopping us from gorging ourselves.

The lesson here is, if you want your family to eat fruit as a snack make sure it is the freshest you can find — farmers' markets are a good place to start looking.

One product which came into our house was a fruit alternative aimed at kids. Pearl picked it up at the supermarket, read the ingredients label and quite rightly ascertained that it was good for her. There were no artificial colours or flavours, no added sugar or preservatives and, as a bonus, it was made in New Zealand.

So every morning she packed the brightly coloured, very cool, pouch into her lunchbox which was sitting right next to a bowl of new season, fresh apples. If she had grabbed an apple she'd get a similar amount of nutrition as this product was mostly apple puree, but there's just something more exciting for kids about packaging which you can take the top off and squeeze into your mouth. Biting an apple just doesn't pack the same interactive buzz.

What Pearl was revealing is what many studies are beginning to say about the ability of children to eat anything which looks like junk food, even when it isn't. In the United States a group of carrot producers packaged their baby carrots in bright, cartoon packaging with the tag line "Eat 'em like junk food" in an effort to get kids to eat carrots. They also produced an accompanying interactive website and video game. It was an immediate hit.

And a 2007 study in *Paediatrics and Adolescent Medicine* found that the more children had been exposed to fast-food marketing, the more they preferred fast food even when the food inside wasn't fast food.

A Californian mandarin producing co-operative has just had huge success in the United States with four TV commercials aimed directly at children, highlighting how easy it is to peel the mandarin, how it has no pips and tastes great. And it seems to be working.

Perhaps there is hope.

My Findings: Chips and Snack Foods

Fruit Hitz

If you compare the nutritional value of one of these 90g pouches with a medium-sized apple, they have similar amounts of protein, carbohydrates and sugars, but the pouch has less fibre, mainly because it doesn't have the skin of the apple included in it. I'm a bit torn about this product. On the one hand, it means my daughter is eating fruit in her lunchbox, because the way it is presented appeals to her. On the other hand, I think children should learn to eat fruit the way nature intended it, in this case, in the shape, texture and feel of an apple. If it helps make up your mind, you can compare the cost of one pouch which is $1.14, to a Royal Gala apple which is about 30c in season.

SUMMARY
- Junk food packaging appeals to children despite the healthy food inside.
- About the same nutritional value as a medium-sized apple but with less fibre.
- Priced at $1.14 per pouch, as opposed to one apple which costs about 30c.

Arnott's Shapes — Pizza

These are perfectly okay for your kids to eat as there seem to be no artificial additives to worry about. Nutritionally they meet the criteria for packaged snack foods as set out by the Healthy Kids Association, which is a non-profit, non-governmental, health promoter based in Australia. Their guidelines advise: fewer than or around 600 kilojoules per serve of snack food — these have 535kj per 25g serve; less than 2g saturated fat — these have 2.7g which isn't bad; and some fibre, about 1g per serve — these have 0.8g. Be aware that there are eight serves in a box, so you wouldn't want your child sitting down and munching through the whole lot in one sitting, which I've seen some of my children do quite easily in the past.

SUMMARY
- No artificial flavours, colours or preservatives.
- Reasonably low in saturated fat.
- Nice to see natural flavours and colours used.

Twisties

The absence of artificial flavourings and colourings separates these from the rest of the packs, but it still takes 17 ingredients to make the product and I would only classify seven as ingredients my Nana would recognise. I would also like to know what oil is used, and I'm not that happy about the additions of MSG and TBHQ which is a preservative which has conflicting studies attached to it. Some say high doses have negative effects on lab animals, such as being precursors to stomach tumours and damage to DNA, and others finding opposite effects. But if you're going to have a processed food snack, it's one of the better choices around.

SUMMARY
- No artificial flavourings or colours.
- Has MSG and TBHQ in it.
- Still takes 17 ingredients, only seven of which Nana would recognise.

ACT II Butter Lover's Flavour Popcorn

In my opinion this popcorn smells artificial and not at all like popcorn cooked with real butter.

SUMMARY
- It's "Butter Lover's" but there's no butter in it.
- Uses palm oil, which is not a popular choice due to its part in deforestation.
- Has added flavourings and colours you won't need if you make it at home.

Ajitsuke Nori (Seaweed Snack)

On the surface, a few strips of innocuous seasoned seaweed seems like an ideal lunchbox inclusion. It is low in fat, low in calories and, importantly, very tasty. It also has iodine which, as New Zealanders, we need to find sources of for our diet, but you don't want to overdo it, especially if your child is eating a lot of bread with iodine in it, food seasoned with iodised salt, or sushi. There are, however, some wonderful other nutrients in here, so I would recommend this as an occasional addition to the lunchbox, though not a daily one.

SUMMARY
- One 16g serving gives you nearly twice the daily iodine recommendation for a child.
- A low-fat, low-calorie, not too salty snack, with lots of essential vitamins and minerals.
- Negligible risk of radioactive contamination.

—my recipes—

Home-made Potato Chips

Unlike most of the recipes in this book this one does take a bit of time. You must never leave the pot of hot oil unattended as it could easily catch alight. Keep children away when cooking these. It is worth using a thermometer as I found keeping an even heat produces the best results.

>Potatoes — Agria are good for chips
>Olive oil — or some people use lard or dripping
>A confectionery thermometer

Wash but do not peel the potatoes . The skins provide extra nutrition. Slice very thinly, using a vegetable peeler. If you are planning to make a lot of these you might want to invest in a mandolin which makes it easier to achieve uniformly thin slices. You want these to be wafer thin. Set out on some paper towels and give them a dab to dry them off.

Heat 10cm depth of oil in the bottom of a large, deep pot. Put in your thermometer and heat until it reaches 180°C. You want to keep it at this heat, and it will go up or down quite quickly so you may need to adjust your element up or down to keep the temperature as even as possible. Put the chips into the oil one by one. Do not overcrowd, you want them to have room to float around a little.

When they are light brown (dark brown tastes a bit bitter) remove with a slotted spoon and drain on some paper towels. When they are all finished and have cooled down sprinkle liberally with salt and serve to an adoring family.

Time taken: 30 minutes to an hour depending on how many you make.

Pita Chips

These are a very healthy alternative to potato chips or corn chips because you use less oil to cook them, they are baked not fried, and they crunch up beautifully. My mother always has a jar of these ready for Pearl when we visit. She makes them and sprinkles them with lemon pepper which makes them taste great.

>3 large pita breads
>½ cup olive oil
>Salt

Brush pita bread with olive oil and sprinkle with salt or lemon pepper seasoning.

Cut each bread into eight triangles. Bake in oven at 200°C for 5–7 minutes. Remove from oven and serve or leave to cool and store in an airtight container.

Time taken: 15 minutes.

Oat Cakes

This recipe is from a book published in 1901 and I have had to adjust it a little for modern kitchens. It features lard, which is animal fat and very hard to get these days, but you can use dripping instead. Most supermarkets and butchers will stock it. In Nana's day she kept a specially designed dripping bowl. It had a lid with holes in it and she would pour the fat from roasts in to collect as much re-usable fat as she could. Butter could be expensive and scarce during the Depression and the two world wars so lard was often used instead to spread on toast and in cooking. Do not even think of substituting the dripping with anything else if you want to be a real Nana.

    2 cups rolled oats
    ½ cup self-raising flour
    2 tsp dripping or lard
    ½ tsp salt
    Boiling water

Mix all of the ingredients except the water in a bowl. Slowly pour on enough boiling water to melt the dripping and form a stiff dough. It should be moist and pliable. On a board covered in more rolled oats, roll out as thin as you can get without it breaking. Cut into squares or use a cookie cutter and cook on a hot griddle or frying pan on both sides until they are golden and crisp. I use dripping to cook them in but you can dry fry them. These go beautifully with cheese or jam and store well in an airtight container.

    Time taken: 30 minutes.

CONCLUSIONS
- Just because a pack of chips says it's Roast Lamb and Mint flavoured does not mean it has any roast lamb or mint in it.
- Despite the fact we have about 100,000 taste buds, they are easily fooled into believing they are eating a strawberry when they're not.
- It takes three ingredients to make a potato chip and two to make a corn chip.
- We are bombarded today with eating guidelines and thousands of products. We were better off in Nana's day when they ate real food, even if there wasn't a lot of it.
- Cheese flavours are often safer in snack foods than other types of flavour as their basis is milk solids, not chemicals.
- Seaweed is a great snack but very high in iodine.
- Fresh fruit of local origin and in season is more likely to be eaten by kids.
- Attractively packaged fruit purees are okay nutritionally but what are they teaching your child about the look and feel of real food?
- Studies have shown that kids will eat real food, like carrots, if it is packaged like junk food.

CHAPTER THREE

milk & other matters

dairy, dairy – quite contrary

I love butter.

There I've said it. Feel free to tell me about its bad fats and how they clog arteries and cause heart attacks. About how anyone with health in mind would ban butter from their diets and replace it with the many wonderful health-giving butter substitutes on the market.

And I'll tell you one thing: "I'd rather eat something which originated in a cow than something which was created in a lab by scientists."

I also know that fats act as carriers for important fat-soluble vitamins A, D, E and K and are needed for the conversion of carotene to vitamin A and for mineral absorption.

And I believe that humans have been eating animal fats for thousands of years, so we are designed to process them. We are not designed to process vegetable oil, which has been chemically altered (hydrogenated), flavoured, coloured, preserved and emulsified into margarine. And up until recently the process of creating margarine created trans fats, which are even worse for you than saturated fat.

Having said that, I eat very little butter. About a teaspoon every day, which I think is okay and some nutritionists agree with me.

Others, like the one who writes for the *NZ Listener* magazine, Jennifer Bowden, don't.

I analysed a table spread, which is what margarine is called these days, and made some points about butter and saturated fat. She wrote in her column:

> *'If you have a family history of heart disease or high cholesterol, avoiding the saturated fat in butter is a good choice,' writes Wendyl Nissen, who then recommends readers make their own spread by mixing butter with olive oil. Contrast this with advice from the National Heart Foundation that everyone should limit their saturated fat intake, irrespective of their family history of heart disease. That means avoiding butter (not mixing it with olive oil) and instead choosing vegetable-oil-based margarines.*

She then attempted to make a point that saturated fats are not required in the diet: "But saturated fatty acids are *not* required in the diet, as our body can synthesise them itself. Hence children do *not* need saturated fat or butter any more than they need chocolate."

She finished rather triumphantly with the statement: "Still, Nissen does us at least one favour, by demonstrating why it's important to question the expertise of anyone offering you nutrition advice."

I have read Bowden's column 10 times and still have no idea what she is talking about, because I'm not a nutritionist, do not understand her language and I'm not sure her readers could either. What comes across in her piece was a hint that she, like many dietitians and nutritionists who have emailed me, feel they should be writing my column.

I explain why that's not such a good idea in Chapter One — Meat.

And let's talk about the National Heart Foundation. They do great work educating people about how to eat for a healthy heart. But as I was writing the column about table spreads I found that the American Heart Foundation allows 16g of saturated fat a day and I read a study which found that there was no clear link between saturated fat consumption and the risk of heart disease. This was not a nutty study, the kind I dismiss when I find them on the internet. It involved the analysis of pooled data from 21 studies that included a total of nearly 348,000 adults. And it was published in the *American Journal of Clinical Nutrition*.

I now know that most nutritionists, unlike Bowden, will not advise that you ban saturated fat completely from your diet because we "don't need it". Instead they suggest you limit it, which makes sense to me.

Now, back to the Heart Foundation. You may remember controversy about the high sugar load of Milo when it was given a Heart Foundation tick as a "healthy choice" food in 2008. Eight months later that tick was removed from Milo's packaging when nutritionists complained that it was 47.6 per cent sugar. This is the tick the Heart Foundation gives to food producers in return for money.

My point here is that not all nutritional advice turns out to be correct. Remember when we were all told not to eat too many eggs because they gave us high cholesterol? Turned out that was not true at all, and in fact eggs are very good for you. Eggs actually contain only 185mg of cholesterol, which is 14 per cent lower than we were previously told. And now an egg a day easily meets dietary guidelines to limit cholesterol consumption to 300 mg a day. Oh, and a large egg actually contains 64 per cent more vitamin D than we were told it did in 2002. One thing no one has changed their mind on is that it still contains 6g of protein.

The saturated fat issue is still being studied, but evidence is emerging that not all saturated fat, nor all foods containing saturated fat should be banned, as other constituents within those foods could be beneficial to heart health. It's complicated.

In the 1990s, when I was editing magazines, a new form of potato chip crossed my desk. It was made with a revolutionary new product called Olestra, a fat substitute that adds no fat, calories, or cholesterol to products and, when used in the production of high-fat foods such as potato chips, lowers the fat content.

I thought this was a marvellous idea and at the office my staff and I munched on them eagerly. But the Olestra bubble was not to last. By the late 1990s some fairly horrific side effects were being felt. Consumers were reporting abdominal cramping and loose stools. Olestra was also discovered to inhibit the absorption of some vitamins and other nutrients. It is now banned in the UK and Canada, and it might as well be here too, as I couldn't find any products listing it among their ingredients.

I mention Olestra as an example of how we can so easily be led to believe that wonderful advances in food science will bring us altered food products which are supposedly better for us, but rarely are.

It's easy to check whether or not the food you are eating is real. If you can trace its origins back to something which started in the soil, i.e. a plant or an animal which ate plants, then you're okay. If you can only trace its origins as far back as a laboratory, you're in trouble.

The best way to eat fat is to drizzle cold-pressed oils, like olive or avocado, onto your bread. Cold-pressed means that the oil hasn't been extracted using chemical solvents which can leave a residue and also reduce its nutritional value.

But every time I try to combine oil with bread I end up pouring too much on or dipping it and eating too much. So I came up with a way to eat oil and butter together by making a spread which I call the Bob Each Way Spread. You get some animal fats but also some health-giving olive oil.

I also believe in some fat for cosmetic reasons. After all, we all have a layer of fat underneath our skin. A study published in the *British Journal of Nutrition* in 2010 looked at the elasticity of the skin of 716 Japanese women and found that those with higher levels of fat (saturated and mono-unsaturated) in their diet had increased levels of skin elasticity.

As you age, I think it makes sense to include fat

in your diet by eating avocados and dipping fresh bread in olive oils and maybe even having a little bit of butter.

One of my colleagues in my magazine editing days used to look at a very skinny woman and mutter: "Eat more pies."

I look at women who have great figures but faces that are wrinkled and drawn and think: "Eat more fat."

I find it incredible that women will ban fat from their diet but be happy to let a cosmetic nurse inject fat deposits into their faces to iron out wrinkles which would probably not be there if they ate enough fat.

In particular, omega-3, which is found in foods such as oily fish, eg salmon, nuts, seeds and flax oil, is known to promote supple skin.

Still, I'm just not sure if an "eat fat and stop the wrinkles" message will ever take off.

I LOVE YOGHURT too. But not the low-fat, artificially flavoured, artificially coloured, highly sweetened or, even worse, artificially sweetened versions most people consume or give their kids.

Real yoghurt has no added sugar and contains lots of wonderful live bacteria, like acidophilus and bifidus, which help our digestive system by maintaining positive bacteria in our gut.

Next time you're at the supermarket, see how much of the shelf is occupied by this sort of yoghurt and then cast your eye across the vast array of flavoured yoghurts packaged in bright eye-catching pottles, including the ones with your kids' favourite cartoon characters. My local supermarket has 62 offerings.

When I looked into a typical one of these yoghurts, Fresh'n'Fruity Berries Galore I grabbed the packet of six fully expecting to find all sorts of nasties in there, but actually they weren't too bad. Apart from the use of artificial flavouring there wasn't a lot wrong with it.

My big take-out from the research around yoghurt was the inability of the customer to know whether the cultures these manufacturers say are in the yoghurt actually are.

Real yoghurt has a shelf life of only about a week, so the challenge for commercial producers is to keep it from going off for a month. The yoghurt that I analysed was bought on September 27 and had a best before date of October 21.

This doesn't mean the yoghurt will have gone off, it just might not taste as good. It's the *use by* date which means you shouldn't eat it after that date as it will have gone off. A lot of people confuse the two terms.

So preservatives must go in, and many commercial yoghurt manufacturers heat it to high temperatures to kill off any bugs. The only problem is that this would also kill off any beneficial live cultures present in the yoghurt.

Acidophilus is a strain of bacteria which has many good health effects, such as encouraging good bacteria in the gut, which is particularly useful after a course of antibiotics, which may have killed off that bacteria. However, much depends on which strain of acidophilus you ingest. Bifidus is a probiotic, which can relieve and treat many intestinal disorders. If you want these beneficial bacteria then you need to buy a yoghurt which clearly states that these bacteria are alive in the yoghurt. And you'll usually only find that information on the packets of the real yoghurts which aren't in the little pottles you feed your kids.

I started making my own yoghurt simply because I found an old yoghurt maker in an op shop one day. I don't have a hot water cupboard, which is the perfect place for yoghurt to mature and bread to rise. So this little plastic contraption was the perfect thing.

Once I had made the yoghurt I never went back. And to be honest I make it more for the hens than for myself. They love it and it's a great source of protein and calcium for them.

MILK USED TO be just milk — delivered to your door in glass bottles every day, fresh as a daisy. If you forgot to put out your empty bottles and tokens you didn't get your milk for breakfast.

It came in one variety, which was pretty much how it came out of the cow, so it had all its fat in it, and to get to the milk you had to scoop out the cream which sat at the top of the bottle.

I would pay a premium price to have that milk back again. Not only would it make better yoghurt and cheese, but I believe it is much better for us, unadulterated and natural.

So what happens to the milk you buy in the supermarket?

First, a high proportion of the cream is separated out, in order to achieve the desired amount of fat you see on the label.

Then they homogenise it, for no other reason that I can find other than to stop the cream rising to the surface like in the old days. So the whole process is to save us having to go to the trouble of shaking the milk or scraping the cream off the top. The majority of our milk goes through this unnecessary process.

It basically involves squirting the milk at high pressure between two hard surfaces. This smashes proteins which contain the natural fat globules and breaks them up so they are dispersed in the milk.

Some people believe this allows the individual milk fat molecules to permeate the stomach/intestinal wall too quickly and enter the blood stream, causing problems with the heart and the circulation system.

I haven't been able to find a study which supports this, but I would still prefer my milk to be unhomogenised.

At present in New Zealand the only brands which are unhomogenised are Sun Latte, Naturalea Organic and Farmhouse (purple packaging with silver top). These are the best milks to make cheese with.

After homogenisation comes pasteurisation, which heats milk to a high temperature to kill any bugs that might be in it. This was a very necessary process when milk-borne diseases like tuberculosis were a threat and hygiene standards in our cow sheds left a lot to be desired. These days, raw milk advocates argue that farmers adhere to very strict hygiene measures and they say that many valuable nutrients are lost in the pasteurisation process. They also say that valuable enzymes which help digest milk are lost — which is why some people cannot tolerate milk — and that valuable bacteria are also killed off.

So by now we are getting milk that is quite heavily processed, but it gets worse. Some milk might be blended with milk permeate which is a waste product of dairy production created by removing all the fat and then concentrating the material that is left. This is a process known as "watering down". It has been revealed in Australia that their major dairy companies often water down their milk, producing a product that sometimes contained as much as 12 per cent of permeate. Farmers claimed it was done by the dairy industry to increase profits, but that was denied at the time.

I have no idea if our milk is watered down in this way, and I am very unlikely to be able to find out. Our food labelling laws are the same as Australia's and there is no legal requirement to disclose permeate on the label.

I know that I have received dozens of emails from people concerned about the quality and taste of their milk and, rather distressingly, the fact that it doesn't curdle like real milk should.

One woman who wrote to me left some blue top milk out on her windowsill to curdle — she was an older woman and liked to use the curds in her cooking. She was distressed because it wouldn't go off.

I haven't had that experience, but I do know that when I was a child the milk arrived in the morning and was heading towards being yoghurt the next day. The milk we buy these days lasts a lot longer.

Some believe this is because it is mixed with the permeate which, because of the lower fat/protein content and increased lactose, does not curdle like milk straight from the cow.

Again, I'm hardly going to get any answers to these questions if I ring up our major dairy producers. It's been hard enough to get them to deal straight with the media about the exorbitant prices they have been charging for the stuff.

If I had a choice, I would buy my milk direct from the cow, and there is quite an underground network which allows you to do that. Legally, a farmer can sell five litres from the gate, and as I'm writing this chapter the Ministry of Agriculture and Forestry has asked for public submissions about whether farmers should be able to sell milk not just from their gate but provide it to urban dwellers as well. I was pleased to see that Federated Farmers supports this move, so it may soon become available to city dwellers like me.

If not, I can join a co-operative whose members take it in turns to go out to a farmer in the country with buckets and deliver the milk to everyone. Or I can drive out there myself every few days. Or I could get a house cow.

Now there's an idea. According to my council bylaws I can keep a goat or a pig or a cow, but I would probably have to let it graze in our local park as my section isn't big enough.

I was quite keen on this idea for quite some time and talked to my friend Carl, who owns a farm up north.

"So what breed do I need to get for maximum milk production?" I asked him.

"How much milk do you think you'll need?" he replied, barely suppressing a smirk.

"Oh, you know, a couple of litres a day, maybe a bit more to make some cheese. I can just smell it now, that wholesome smell of milk from my childhood," I said, gazing into space.

"Well, most cows will give you 15 litres a day," he said, sitting back as he took a sip of wine and stared at me over the rim of his glass.

"Did you say 15 litres?" I said, incredulous. "That's about two buckets full."

"And you have to milk her every morning and every night, if she'll let you," he chuckled. "Have you ever milked a cow before?"

"Not exactly."

"It's quite an art and some cows just don't like you squeezing them if you don't know what you're doing."

"Right," I said, slowly absorbing the reality of having a house cow.

"Oh, and all that travel you do overseas? You'll have to find someone who's prepared to do the milking for you, which in your neighbourhood of artists, writers and media personalities shouldn't be too difficult."

He was now openly guffawing and insisting that

everyone else at the table be included in our conversation.

"Okay, I get it," I said to shut him up. "No house cow!"

But I will have my house cow. Just when I finally get my few acres in the country and some friendly neighbours who might like to share her and her milk.

MANY PEOPLE ARE allergic to dairy products and three of my children have to limit their intake but can eat them in moderation. My daughter Hannah has given them up completely and now eats a vegan diet, which means she only consumes plant foods. So no eggs, dairy, chicken, fish or meat.

I got the idea to look at soy milk when cartons of it kept appearing in my fridge.

The only time I had ever tasted soy milk was when I went to interview musician Jools Topp of the Topp Twins shortly after she had been diagnosed with breast cancer. The always hospitable twins offered me a coffee and I accepted gratefully.

When it arrived I took a sip and nearly spat the whole lot out.

"That'll be the soy milk," Lynda Topp laughed. "We're not doing dairy now. We're eating good food. For Jools," she explained.

"Good oh," I said and pretended to have a few more sips before abandoning it for the remainder of the interview.

To me it tastes really, really horrible. But Hannah tells me that you get used to it, especially in coffee. I did once use it in a vegan chocolate cake I made and it was fine, so I'm keeping an open mind. And Hannah tells me almond milk tastes a lot better if I ever want to give up the dairy.

The thing about soy milk is that it is a highly processed food. It's not technically a milk, because by definition milk is the substance which is produced by mammals and comes out of their udders. So it really should be called soy imitation milk or soy juice. And, rather ironically for a substance consumed and loved by healthy eaters, it is the epitome of a processed food, something which transforms a food item into another form. To make a milk out of soybeans you need to soak dry soybeans then grind them with water. The result is then heated to improve the flavour and sterilise it.

Soy milk drinkers emailed me because they were concerned soy milk had sugar added into it. But they needn't have worried. It did, but per serve there wasn't as much sugar as there is in cow's milk.

What it did have added to it was the vitamins you would normally find in cow's milk, plus flavour. It also had about the same amount of protein as milk.

There are two concerns with soy milk. One is making sure that it is GM free, which basically means that the genes of soybeans have not been altered either to perform better or, in the case of America, given a gene which made them resistant to the herbicide Roundup. Many people oppose genetically modified foods because of the risk to biodiversity and the unknown effects on humans.

The second concern is the phytoestrogens. Soybeans are rich in phytoestrogens, which are estrogen-like substances found in some plants. Some health advocates fear that these substances could interfere with a child's development and even cause early puberty, thyroid problems, breast development in males, or other difficulties. The New Zealand Ministry of Health does not recommend soy-based formula for general use in infant feeding because the long-term effects of phytoestrogens in soy-based formula as an infant's main food source are not known.

Know Your Fats

Most health advice is to eat between 20–30g of fat a day to maintain good health. By the way, your brain is 60 per cent fat and without adequate amounts of fat in the diet fat-soluble vitamins such as A and E can't pass through the intestinal walls. Working out which fats are good for you and why is a very confusing process. Believe me, I still have to remind myself. Here is a brief and hopefully easy to understand guide to fats:

Saturated Fat
This is found in animal fats, such as butter and meat, as well as some tropical oils. Your body can also make them from carbohydrates.

Trans Fats
When margarine was first used the manufacturers needed to make the vegetable oils they used solid at

room temperature. They did this by firing hydrogen at the oil (hydrogenation), which formed trans fats. These have been found to increase the incidence of cardiovascular disease. During the past decade, margarine makers have made an effort to decrease trans fat levels. Some trans fats occur naturally in ruminants' stomachs but the quantities are small.

Polyunsaturated Fat
This is good fat. It helps your body get rid of newly formed cholesterol so it keeps the blood cholesterol level down and reduces cholesterol deposits in artery walls. Polyunsaturated fat can be found mostly in nuts, seeds, fish, algae, leafy greens, and krill. Whole food sources are always best, as processing and heating may damage polyunsaturated fats.

Mono-unsaturated Fat
Recent research has shown that mono-unsaturated fats may also help reduce blood cholesterol, as long as the diet is very low in saturated fat. It is the main component in olive oil, and present in almonds, pecans, cashews, peanuts and avocados.

Omega-3 and omega-6 — which one do I need? Not a lot of people actually understand the omegas, but omega-3 is dotted liberally over much of our labelling as an enticement to buy.

Put simply we need two types of polyunsaturated fats — omega-3 and omega-6 fatty acids. We can't produce them ourselves and they are both required for lots of body functions, but the list of benefits from eating enough omega 3 is as long as your arm. It can prevent depression, obesity, asthma, diabetes, high blood pressure, cancer, attention deficit disorder, rheumatoid arthritis and heart disease. Oh, and it can lower cholesterol.

If you're interested in looking good, omega-3 will also promote healthy hair and hair growth and supple, youthful skin.

But the two need to be kept in balance — preferably no higher than four omega-6 to one omega-3. It is thought that in our Stone Age years the amount of each was equal and in a traditional Greek diet it is fewer than two omega-6 to one omega-3.

It may not surprise you to learn that in the modern diet the ratio can be as high as 20 omega-6 to one omega-3.

The problem is that omega-3 is hard to come by in the diets we eat today. You can find it in flax oil, nuts, seeds, fish, seafood, egg yolks and good quality, grass-fed (which is the case in New Zealand) beef. I like to eat salmon once a week as just one 100g piece is about the size and thickness of a deck of cards and contains about 2,000mg omega-3s.

Nutritionists recommend about 650mg of omega-3s a week for women and 1,100mg for men.

We need to eat less omega-6 yet it is really easy to find in foods such as margarine and most cooking oils. The fact that our omegas are so out of balance in our modern diets is being blamed on the big increase of consumption in margarine, which people buy and eat because they are advised that it is good for heart health.

My Findings: Dairy and Substitutes

Home Brand Table Spread

Margarine came into popularity during World War II as a cheaper substitute for butter, but more recently it has become popular as a healthier alternative. Health authorities have recommended that people switch from butter to margarine to avoid saturated fat intake and protect themselves from heart disease. We are encouraged to lower our cholesterol by choosing plant oils (margarine) over animal fats (butter). Yet this spread contains nine ingredients (some artificial) designed to make it taste, look and feel like butter.

SUMMARY
- Contains colour and flavour to help it taste like butter.

- Takes nine ingredients to make the spread, as opposed to three for butter.
- Uses plant oils, but we don't know which ones.

Fresh'n'Fruity Berries Galore Low Fat Yoghurt

Most yoghurts marketed for children will now feature no artificial flavours or colours, but they still have quite a lot of sugar added to dull the naturally tart taste of real yoghurt. Yoghurts intended for adults do not have so many assurances. I am pleasantly surprised to see that the manufacturers resisted the urge to make it strawberry pink by adding a colouring.

SUMMARY
- To avoid artificial additives go for yoghurts aimed at children.
- Probiotics may be present in the yoghurt but they might not be alive. Check labels for "live cultures".
- It takes 11 ingredients to make what is basically fermented milk with fruit.

So Good — Regular

I know many people prefer not to consume dairy products because of lactose intolerance or simply because they prefer not to eat animal products full stop. This product does its best to imitate milk, but still carries a risk of being high in phytoestrogens, and no one is quite sure what that means for us while we wait for further research. Soymilk is a processed food and a milk substitute, but it can bring relief to many people.

SUMMARY
- Safe for vegans as no animal products are used.
- Sugar is added for flavour, but cow's milk has more sugar.
- Uses non GM soybeans.

—my recipes—

Home-made Butter

>Salt (optional)
>600ml cream

Simply pour the cream into a bowl, get out your electric beaters and whisk until lumps of butter appear and eventually form one big lump. This takes about five minutes on a medium speed. Remove the lump of butter and put it in a bowl of cold water, squeezing gently. Rinse under a running tap and then put in a bowl and use. Add salt to taste. (It will also last a bit longer with salt in it)

>*The liquid left in the bowl after the butter has

appeared is called buttermilk and makes scones very light and delicious if you use it instead of milk in your usual recipe.

Time taken: 10 minutes.

Herb Butter

Soften 100g of your freshly made butter and mix into it 2 tbsp of freshly chopped herbs, such as chives, parsley and thyme mixed together. You could also use basil, mint or rosemary, but separately, not together. Finish off with a few drops of lemon juice mixed in and then roll into a sausage shape, wrap in greaseproof paper, fold the ends as you would a Christmas cracker and refrigerate. When you need it simply remove from the fridge and slice off a piece.

Time taken: 5 minutes.

Brandy Butter

Take 100g of your freshly made butter. Soften and stir in 100g of icing sugar and then stir in 3 tbsp of brandy which you add gradually (you can also use rum). Put the butter in attractive little dishes on the table when you serve hot puddings or desserts.

Time taken: 5 minutes.

Anchovy Butter

This is a very old recipe from my 1845 cookbook *Modern Cookery for Private Families* by Eliza Acton. It was very popular served with roast beef, fried fish or even fresh radishes. In Nana's day they would have had to skin and bone tiny anchovy fillets, but these days we can buy them ready to go in tins or jars.

To 100g of your butter (made without salt) mash in eight anchovies, and a pinch each of nutmeg, cayenne and mace. Roll up as with the herb butter and keep in the fridge. Some more modern recipes also add 1 tsp of finely chopped capers.

Time taken: 5 minutes.

Bob Each Way Spread

Mix together equal quantities of butter and olive oil. Say 250g of butter, topped up to 500g weight on your kitchen scales with olive oil. Heat gently for a moment to soften the butter so that you can mix it into the oil. Do not let it cook! This spread gives you the combined nutrition of both butter and olive oil, reduces the amount of saturated fats and is spreadable straight from the fridge. (Do keep in the fridge or it will get too soft at room temperature.) You can use better quality butter and olive oil, but the more virgin the oil the more it will taste like olive oil rather than butter and the greener it will look. Sometimes this will separate because it contains no emulsifiers, in which case you just need to warm it slightly to recombine.

Time taken: 10 minutes.

Home-made Yoghurt

If you can find a yoghurt maker in an op shop this will be much easier. The yoghurt makers are insulated containers in which you place your yoghurt to culture at an even temperature for six or seven hours.

Otherwise you can wrap it in blankets or towels and put in a warm place like a hot water cupboard.

> 4 tbsp live culture yoghurt — check it has live cultures such as acidophilus and is not sweetened. It should be tart tasting and have lots of lumps in it
>
> 900ml warm milk — try to use unhomogenised
>
> 2 tbsp whole milk powder — this is optional, but it does make the result a bit thicker

Heat the milk to scalding to kill off unwanted bacteria and then allow to cool to lukewarm. Mix in the yoghurt and the milk powder. Place in your yoghurt maker or wrap in blankets immediately, and in six hours you should have some lovely, healthy, live culture yoghurt. When you begin to run out, save 4 tbsp and make another batch.

Mix this yoghurt with honey, mashed up banana, fruit puree or even a little bit of jam for your kids.

Time taken: 10 minutes plus proving time.

Vegan Beetroot Chocolate Cake

> 3 cups flour
>
> 2 cups sugar
>
> 6 tbsp cocoa
>
> 2 tsp baking soda
>
> 1 tsp salt
>
> 1 med sized beetroot
>
> 2 cups water
>
> ¾ cup vegetable oil
>
> 2 tbsp vinegar
>
> 2 tsp vanilla essence or extract

Preheat oven to 180°C. Sift dry ingredients together in a large bowl. Grate and mix in the beetroot. Make a well and add the wet ingredients. Mix until an even batter forms without lumps.

Bake for 40 minutes in a greased cake tin. Let cake rest for 5-10 minutes before turning out onto a wire rack.

Chocolate Ganache

- ⅓ cup milk alternative (I used soy)
- 2 tbsp margarine
- 1 cup dairy-free chocolate chips (bulk-bin chocolate chips at New World and Pak n' Save are vegan, otherwise check the packet — most dark chocolates are okay)

Using the double boiling method (ingredients in a heat-proof bowl, sat inside a pot of boiling water), heat the 'milk' and margarine until the margarine is melted.

Add the chocolate chips. Stir continuously until the chips are completely melted and the mixture is very smooth.

Time Taken: 1 ½ hours.

Conclusions

- We are designed to eat animal fats.
- Saturated fat should be limited but not deleted from your diet, especially children's diets.
- Butter tastes amazing and a little goes a long way.
- Margarine is oils made solid with added colour, flavouring, preservatives and emulsifiers.
- If you're going to eat yoghurt, make sure you are getting the benefits of live cultures, not ones killed off by heating.
- Soy milk is a processed food which really should be called "juice" or "imitation milk".
- It's really easy to make your own butter, spread and yoghurt, so give it a try and cut out the additives.
- Get a house cow if you can.

CHAPTER FOUR

dips & spreads

all part of the process

It wasn't much of a summer down at the caravan. Our years of long, hot days filled with sunshine had made this our favourite place to be from Christmas Day until school returned in early February.

But not this year. Winds, howling rain and the need to wear jumpers in the middle of summer had made us all a bit grumpy. Except Pearl.

Finally old enough, at nearly 14, this was the first summer she was spending in her own tent, with her friend Tulip. The two of them spent most of their time hooting with laughter and scoffing the impressive array of junk food they had collected for feasts.

When it comes to Pearl and junk food, I have never prevented her from eating it. There is no surer way to set up a craving for a certain food than to ban it. I know from experience that the minute I tell myself I can't have any chocolate, that's all I can think about for the rest of the day, and I always end up eating some.

I also don't want Pearl to be one of those kids

who hide food from me or turn up at friends' houses and raid their pantries for the forbidden treats.

What I try to do is teach her a bit about what she eats. To look at labels and read them. To question any food ingredient she can't pronounce. To ask me to help her interpret the many ways food manufacturers find to hide the names of chemicals beneath a series of codes.

I like to think I've just been a gentle guide through the confusing process of helping her work out what she was putting in her stomach, but I know that hasn't been the case.

There were times when our normally enjoyable trips to the supermarket together were marred by my insistence in picking up every item she put in the trolley and analysing it for her, there and then.

"Enough, already," she would snap.

Then there were what became known as the "dinner lectures" where I would sit down fresh from writing one of my columns and bore the pants off everyone about a preservative I had just found in a family favourite, or a colouring which was banned in a number of countries.

"Enough already," the whole family would snap.

In the 1980s when I raised my older two children, there were no such lectures, and they got to eat whatever they wanted. My son Daniel, in particular, had a penchant for anything blue. Blue milk, blue soft drink, blue lollies. He and his sister Hannah were both asthmatics, and I now know that the artificial colouring Brilliant Blue, which is still used today in many foods for children, should be avoided by asthmatics. I could have done a better job of monitoring their junk food intake.

So, in some ways, Pearl is my "mea culpa" child. My attempt to do a better job.

Now, I don't lecture, I just wait until Pearl asks a question while holding up a processed food.

"It seems okay, but what do you think?" she'll say, and so I'll scan the three letter codes and give her a quick appraisal. Most of the time her instincts are pretty spot on.

And occasionally I'll tell her it's not that great, and she'll say, "I don't care, everyone has them at school, can I just try them?"

And I'll let her. I notice she never buys another one though.

Over the years, Pearl has slowly weaned herself away from some of the worst foods by choice. Once she knew what was in some of them, she just didn't want to eat them and then she began to taste and differentiate between real food and false food.

"There's something in this which tastes really nice," she will say as she munches into a stuffed Indian roti, which I buy at the local Indian food supply shop to keep in the freezer. She'll grab one and fry it up for a snack after school. Consequently she now knows what fenugreek, cumin and coriander taste like and enjoys a wider range of flavours.

Her favourite snacks are cheese and crackers, hummus and corn chips and she has been known to eat five bananas in one sitting. That was during one of her terrifyingly sudden growth spurts, the kind most 14-year-olds are prone to.

So back at the camp, when I noticed bags of processed food disappearing into the girls' tent I wasn't too concerned. If it's anything like any of Pearl's other feasts with her girlfriends it will be a temporary aberration and will most probably end with half of it being rejected because it "tastes terrible after the first few bites".

As I stumbled off to the ablution block the next morning, I tripped over a jar of something green I had become very familiar with while writing my column.

It was a guacamole dip, and it lay on its back, unopened and rejected from the tent of feasts.

I left it there, momentarily worried about the waste of having it exposed to the sun.

When the girls got up I asked them why the dip had met such a nasty end.

"Tulip bought it, and I told her it only has 4 per cent avocado, so we decided not to eat it," said Pearl.

"I had no idea," said Tulip as if she was talking about the recent overdose of a Hollywood celebrity. "Mum will be horrified."

And so the jar lay there for the rest of the holiday, slowly getting less bright green as a symbol of teenage revolt.

"We could give it to someone in the camp who isn't a member of the food police," suggested Paul.

"You can't knowingly give junk food to someone," I said.

"But it's a waste."

He had a point.

What wasn't a waste was the food items the girls chose a few days later when we went into town to replenish the supplies we were making our way through with alarming speed as a way of easing our disappointment at the terrible weather and the absence of anything resembling a summer.

I decided to conduct my own personal experiment and let them go for it.

"You can choose anything you like for your tent feasts," I said generously.

I would like to report that they loaded the trolley down with fresh fruit, raw yoghurt and fruit juice. What they actually found was camembert cheese, crackers, hummus, Coke, lollies and three gossip magazines.

"Camembert?" I said, picking up the soft rounds of creamy cheese.

"WE LOVE CAMEMBERT!" they shouted in unison.

They were big city kids whose parents had served camembert hundreds of times as they were growing up.

I was impressed at their refined tastes and mentally had a brief nutrition versus cost argument in my head. The camembert cost $5 plus the crackers which came in at $3. That was a snack which would last them two sittings I reasoned and give them some good nutrition in the form of protein from the cheese. There was also a bit of fat, but they were growing girls.

"Better that than a couple of packets of

chemically flavoured chips and a bottle of chemically flavoured and coloured soft drink to wash it down," I said to my husband. "Costs the same."

Pearl also loves goat's feta, but that does get a bit expensive.

The hummus I was absolutely delighted about because it is made out of chickpeas, which are one of nature's great foods, being high in protein and fibre as well as providing lots of iron and other minerals. Kids love chickpeas when they are whipped up into a hummus.

As for the Coke — we look at that in Chapter 10: Drink but both girls are also big water drinkers, so this was definitely a treat as were the lollies.

I had one suggestion to make.

"How about some juice, a bunch of bananas and some grapes?"

I knew they would both enjoy those and I had managed to sneak some fruit into the equation.

WHEN I WAS a child there wasn't much to offer in the way of dips except the classic Kiwi onion soup dip. This was considered quite the thing at my parents' dinner parties to serve with drinks before dinner. My mother's cookbook from that era lists under "Cocktail Snacks" bacon and dates (grilled), stuffed eggs, liver sausage pate, chicken liver pate (Cordon Bleu) and bacon and parsley savouries. There is no recipe for the thousands of cheese straws I made for my mother's dinner parties, because that was in my head.

The onion soup dip made a huge comeback

during the 2011 Rugby World Cup when Kiwis found themselves in front of the television watching the game and reaching for packets of chips and dip.

Shortly before we went camping I looked at it for my column and discovered that it wasn't too bad for you. So guess what I was serving as my treat most nights at wine o'clock?

A close relative to the dip is the spread which we put on toast or crackers for breakfast or a snack. Most New Zealand households have peanut butter and a yeast spread, such as Marmite, in their pantries. Some people think peanut butter is too high in fat to be healthy, but you don't need a lot, and you are eating some fat from nuts, which is good for your body due to the high levels of mono-unsaturated fat (just like that in olive oil). Peanut butter also provides protein and folate. But not all peanut butters are the same, because some add sugar, as well as cheaper oils than the natural peanut oil, which is produced by grinding peanuts, and emulsifiers to stop the oil settling in the top of the jar. Nuts are both naturally sweet and oily, so I don't understand why producers feel the need to add sugar and oil.

One brand, Kraft Light Crunchy Peanut Spread, has only 63 per cent of peanuts in a 375g jar and six added ingredients, including sugar, maltodextrin (a form of sugar), salt, vegetable oil, an antioxidant and an emulsifier. Compare this to peanut butter made yourself for which you have only one ingredient — peanuts.

You can also make a range of other nut butters

which your family will love, such as almond butter, macadamia nut butter or cashew butter.

Possibly the most Kiwi of spreads is Marmite, which has the Australian cousin Vegemite. These spreads are high in folate and B12 and are great on toast for a hangover, but they too have succumbed to the demands of food processing. When I was a child Marmite tasted completely different and also had a different, almost treacle-like, consistency. But then it was reformulated and a close look at the ingredients label for Marmite reveals added sugar in two forms, salt in two forms and colour. Vegemite has similar ingredients, but does not add any sugar.

This is very different from the Marmite we used to eat. I know this because for the past four years I've been buying and eating British-produced Marmite, which is marketed here under the brand name Our Mate. You'll find it on the shelf next to Marmite and Vegemite, in a little old-fashioned jar. It has a lovely, black, treacle-like consistency, just as I remember and tastes just like it used to. Its ingredients? Nothing but yeast extract, salt, some vegetable extracts and similar vitamins as the other two spreads. I much prefer eating something without colouring and sugar.

I don't have a recipe for making your own yeast spread, but you can buy savoury yeast flakes at some health stores. These are delicious sprinkled on buttered toast or on top of soups. I also make a very nice dairy-free pesto using them (recipe below).

My Findings: Dips & Spreads

Signature Range Guacamole Creamy Dip

- Contains only 4 per cent avocado
- Six real foods included (onion, capsicum, canola oil, avocado, garlic and lemon juice concentrate).
- 14 additives, including emulsifiers, fillers, thickeners, preservatives, colours and added sugar.

Kiwi Dip — Nestlé Reduced Cream and Maggi Onion Soup Mix

- 38 per cent less fat than a dip using full cream.
- Artificial flavour, but no artificial colours or preservatives.
- Onion soup component contains MSG.

—my recipes—

Guacamole

    Avocado
    Lemon juice
    Tomato
    Garlic

Mash up an avocado, stir in the juice of a lemon, 1 chopped tomato and 1 tsp finely chopped garlic. It will cost about the same as a bought dip, although considerably less in summer, when avocados are in season. Additives: nil.

    Time taken: Five minutes.

Onion Dip

    250ml can reduced cream
    1 packet onion soup
    1 tsp vinegar or lemon juice

Mix together cream and soup till smooth. Stir in vinegar or juice and leave in the fridge until set.

    Time taken: Two minutes.

Hummus

    1 x 400g can chickpeas
    2 tbsp olive oil (or avocado oil)
    2 cloves garlic finely chopped
    1 lemon

salt and pepper

Drain the chickpeas and put in your food processor. Add the olive oil, chopped garlic, juice of the lemon and some salt and pepper. Process until smooth. To add extra flavour you can mix in chopped herbs, such as parsley, or some feta with some finely chopped fresh mint, or a little chilli with a sprinkle of cumin and coriander powder.

Time taken : Five minutes.

Pea and Lemon Dip

Kids love this dip and it's a great way to get some veges into them without them noticing.

- 1½ cups frozen peas, just cooked until they are bright green
- 2 tsp lemon juice
- ⅓ cup cream cheese
- 1 garlic clove, crushed
- ¼ cup chopped fresh mint
- Salt and pepper to taste

Put the cooked peas, lemon juice, cream cheese, garlic, mint and salt and pepper in your food processor and whizz until combined. Try to leave a bit of texture in there. Put in a bowl and drizzle with a little good quality olive oil before serving.

Time taken: 20 minutes.

Smashed Chickpea and Avocado Dip

- 1 x 400g can chickpeas
- 1 ripe avocado

¼ cup fresh coriander
2 tbsp finely chopped spring onions
Juice of a lime
Salt and pepper to taste

Rinse and drain the chickpeas and put in a bowl. Using a potato masher, mash up the chickpeas with the avocado. Or you can whizz it up in a food processor.

Add the lime juice, coriander, spring onions and salt and pepper to taste.

Time taken: Five minutes.

Peanut Butter

2 cups shelled peanuts
salt

Place the peanuts in a 180°C oven until roasted and lightly browned (about 10 minutes). Rub off the red husk in a tea-towel and put them through a hand mincer two or three times, or blend in your food processor until a smooth mass. This can take as along as 10 minutes to release the oils in the nuts. Flavour with salt and store in airtight jars.

Nut Butter

2 cups roasted and shelled, unsalted almonds,
    macadamia nuts or cashews
salt

You can usually buy nuts roasted and with no salt added in the supermarkets or health shops. Or you can buy them raw and roast them yourself in a 150°C oven in a single layer for about 20 minutes. Keep an eye on them and take them out as soon as they smell cooked and look golden.

Tip the nuts (cool first if you have roasted them) into a food processor. I find a small bowl is best. Process until they reach a powdery stage, and then they will release their oils and turn into butter. Depending on the nuts you may have to add just a little peanut oil to get the right consistency for a spreadable butter, but you shouldn't need to.

Add salt if you like, but, again, you don't really need to.

Keep in an air-tight jar and store in the fridge as your nut butter doesn't have preservatives. It should last about a month.

Time taken: 5 minutes.

Time taken if roasting required: 25 minutes.

Dairy-free Pesto

1½ cups fresh basil
⅓ cup olive oil
1 cup pine nuts toasted in a pan
5 cloves garlic
⅓ cup nutritional yeast or yeast flakes
salt and pepper

Put all the ingredients in your food processor and combine until you still have a few lumps but they are well blended together. Taste and add salt and pepper to your liking. This stores well in your fridge in a glass jar.

CONCLUSIONS
- The key to getting kids to eat less junk food is not to ban it but let them eat it as a treat.
- While they're choosing or eating it, talk to them in a non-confrontational way about what is in it and examine labels together.
- When they are eating healthy foods, reinforce them and talk to them about what is good for them in it. "Hey that orange is giving you heaps of vitamin C," is a good one, or "I can really taste these corn chips now that we've got the ones without the chemical flavourings on them."
- It takes five minutes to make a dip free of additives.

CHAPTER FIVE

breakfast

just for starters

"Can I look at that, Grandma?" says our four-year-old grand-daughter, Lila, as I'm putting the shopping in the back of the Prius. We have just made our way around the supermarket and Lila has been a great help.

"Look at what?" I say, as we both gaze at the bags of shopping.

"That one there," she says pointing at a brightly coloured box.

"Oh, that's not for you," I say reaching in and covering the offending piece of garish marketing with a bag of potatoes.

"Why not?" she says, disappointed.

"That's for Grandma's work," I reply and hastily strap her into her car seat. "When Grandma has done her work on it, maybe you can have one next time you visit."

Most visits to the supermarket require that I look for products that I can review in my column. This box was for some brightly coloured biscuits called Oki Doki Disco Bits. They looked frightening in terms of artificial colours and so I threw them in the trolley. Lila never said a word when I took them off the shelf, nor to my knowledge even noticed they were in the trolley. But when it comes to kid marketing Lila is a perfect target. She has an innate ability to seek and find any brightly coloured foods within a 10-metre radius.

I'm not sure what she thinks Grandma does when she "works" on these foods but she knows that they generally live on a shelf in my office, lined up and waiting for my magnifying glass to hover critically over their ingredients panel.

I know Lila knows this because it's her first stop at every visit, once we have all been greeted with a cuddle, she's patted our dog, Shirl, and gone out to check that her white hen, who she has named "Mummy", is still around.

I had an extremely colourful and enticing box of Kellogg's Fruit Loops sitting in my office when Lila came to visit recently. She regards my office as our "second" kitchen because on any occasion she might find all sorts of wonderful foods lined up on my shelf ready to be analysed for the column. I was in the "first" kitchen, when she appeared clutching the box of Froot Loops with a look of wonderment on her face.

"Grandma, can I please have these in a bowl with some milk?"

Something about the packaging had managed to tell her that a) she desperately needed to eat these and b) it was a food you had in a bowl with milk.

"Why do you want them?" I asked.

"They look nice," was all she said.

I gently pried them off her with promises of other treats and hid them in the pantry.

When I went back to get them to write about, I found that my 26-year-old son, Daniel, had succumbed to the same marketing message, but didn't need to ask first, and ate them.

I am always astonished at the power of packaging and its ability to transfix a small child or her uncle. Lila lives in a household where her parents are very aware of food additives and eat a very healthy, real-food diet. (Not because I pressured them —they are just intelligent consumers, honestly.)

So Lila's exposure to junk food and the bright packaging is minimal and she would have had no conditioning to tell her that inside these packets are sweet tasting, moreish foods. She just wouldn't know. Yet something about the design of the boxes sets off a reaction in her brain which gives her the drive to search for it in bags of shopping or reach up onto a shelf and carry it all the way down the hall to me in the kitchen.

It is no secret that kids as young as Lila are directly targeted by advertising, not just on TV but also techniques such as free gifts, competitions, games and puzzles, website games and movie promotions.

And that marketing is why breakfast becomes a minefield for well meaning parents to negotiate.

Next time you are at the supermarket, wander down the breakfast aisle and take note of the packaging. It all looks fantastic. Aside from the relentless use of every bright colour in the rainbow, you will see three elements competing for your attention: chocolate, punchy bright berries and fruit and fibre.

In my house over the years, we have been through most of the cereal crazes as each of our five children has begged to be allowed a new brand and their busy working mum (former) bought them.

Have you ever noticed Jerry Seinfeld's cereal shelf in the kitchen on *Seinfeld*? Next time you watch the show have a look. One internet source sets the number at nine, mostly cornflakes and shredded wheat. His cereal shelf looks exactly how ours looked for years, as every child claimed a new brand as theirs.

While you're in the breakfast cereal aisle, see if you can find one box which lists the sugar content per 100g at less than 15g, which is what we should aim for when buying our kids cereal.

Consumer magazine conducted a survey of our breakfast cereals in 2008 and found that seven products had more than 40 per cent sugar — over three teaspoons in a 30g serve. I've listed them at the end of the chapter for you, in case they're sitting on your Seinfeld cereal shelf. One of them is the aforementioned Kellogg's Froot Loops which I prevented Lila from eating.

My focus when first studying this cereal was primarily on the three artificial colours used in it (see my findings below) but then I worked out that, if Lila had been allowed her Froot Loops with milk, she would have consumed 4.3 teaspoons of sugar in her bowl.

I can guarantee you will not find a box of cereal

in the supermarket with low sugar until you come to Weet-Bix. Plain old Weet-Bix is the star of the cereal aisle, at just 2.8g per 100g. Admittedly, a lot of people add sugar, but at least you can control that and most kids enjoy eating them.

Lila eats two "bix" for breakfast every morning and won't be swayed from them even when her grandpa is offering to make her sausages and eggs.

My mother, Elis, however, can't stand them. Something to do with trying to avoid eating them when she was a child by sneezing into them, thinking her parents would deem that a reasonable enough excuse not to have to eat them. But no. She had to eat every last bit and has never touched them since.

As a guide, when you are out shopping, if sugar appears in the ingredients list directly under the name of the cereal, such as rice, corn or wheat, that means that the second biggest ingredient in there is sugar, and you should put it straight back on the shelf.

The other thing you need to think about is salt levels (fewer than 400mg sodium per 100g of cereal) and fibre.

We all know that we don't get enough fibre in our diets. It's good for bowel health and digestion and the things that give you fibre — fresh fruit, veges and wholegrains — tend to be really nutritious and good for you. Unfortunately, I've noticed a trend for food manufacturers to add what I call "faux fibre" to their processed foods, using vegetable gums and inulin, which is a substance that occurs naturally in root vegetables, particularly chicory. Other additions include polydextrose, which is created out of dextrose (glucose), sorbitol, a low-calorie carbohydrate, and citric acid to add to processed foods, usually to provide fibre. It is called a functional fibre because no one knows if it has the same health benefits as fibre found in real foods.

A good guide for children's fibre requirements is 5g to 15g per 100g, so look out for that on the label, and if you see inulin or vegetable gum in the ingredients panel, reject it in favour of something which uses wholegrains and fruit to provide fibre.

Another problem with most breakfast cereals is the fact that they are extruded. This means perfectly good wholegrains are ground up, made into a slurry with liquid, heated to high temperatures, then pressurised through small holes to create shapes such as rings, flakes or puffs. You have to wonder just how much nutrition gets killed off in the process with those high heats and pressures.

OFTEN WHEN I'M out and about, people like to talk about the food column and what it has taught them.

"Thank goodness Krispies are okay," said my aunt. "They're my favourite biscuit."

"I haven't touched a raspberry jam slice since the day I read your column," said a woman I met at a knitting bee.

And, of course, many people have suggestions for foods I should look at. By far the most disturbing conversation along these lines was with a woman I was doing some work with.

"I have this friend who basically throws those cartons of Up&Go at her kids from dawn until dusk," she said. "That's all they eat. For breakfast they sit there in the car sucking on them on their way to school, they have another one with their lunch and sometimes dinner too. I've tried to tell her they need some real food but she believes they are good for them. Are they?"

Then I got the emails about Up&Go: "My kids have one every day and I'm wondering how healthy they are," said one mother.

"I really don't like this product because it has so much sugar and it's like giving your child a milkshake for breakfast," said another.

I was well acquainted with Up&Go. My son Daniel has never been a great breakfast eater, and so for a while he took one of these with him but in the end he didn't even eat those, claiming the texture was weird.

Up&Go, for those who are not familiar with it, is a drink which is endorsed by the All Blacks in its advertising campaign and claims on the box to have "the protein, energy and dietary fibre of 2 Weet-Bix and milk".

It is reasonable that parents like myself would read that and presume that in the little box we are handing over to our kids is simply two Weet-Bix and some milk all mashed up. And presumably it would have the same nutritional benefits.

Wrong.

The label should also state that it has 11.7g more sugar and 13 more ingredients than a simple bowl of Weet-Bix and milk. By the time I'd finished writing the column I was quite angry with Sanitarium for the misconception and wrote: "Is it really that hard to get a kid to sit down at the kitchen table and eat solid food these days? Are we raising a nation of astronauts in training who need to develop a taste for liquid food?"

I think if you've got a kid who needs something quick to eat in the car you can throw them a banana. And if you've got a kid who only likes to drink their meals, whip up a smoothie, put it in a bottle and let them drink that. On the Sanitarium website they even recommend that you throw a Weet-Bix into the smoothies.

I also took a look at Nestlé Milo Oats, mainly because Pearl had picked them up in the supermarket and loved them. I'm a big fan of oats, as not only are they a good source of fibre but they also do wonderful soothing things to your digestive system.

Nestlé have a range of breakfast cereals marketed under the Milo name and some are better than others. Milo Oats is a better one.

I found that they weren't too high in sugar and were a good source of fibre. I saw them as a great food to get kids interested in porridge for breakfast. I also found a study which showed that children who had oats for breakfast had better spatial memory (which means being able to remember geographical details like the interior of your house), better short-term memory and better listening attention than children who ate ready-to-eat cereal or no breakfast at all. Pearl was very relieved.

PUTTING THE CHOICE of cereal for your kids aside, there is a bigger problem emerging on the horizon for families, and that's the kid who just won't eat breakfast. This is cause for concern because every study you read emphasises the importance of breakfast for kids to kickstart their brains and give them the energy to see them through a day of learning at school.

One University of Sydney study, conveniently commissioned by Kellogg's, looked at the type of breakfast eaten by 800 New South Wales children aged eight to 16, across 19 different schools. The students who ate breakfast before their tests performed better, and those who ate the most nutritious breakfasts, such as cereal and milk, or eggs on toast, got the highest scores. They also scored higher on literacy and numeracy tests than their classmates who ate only toast.

It is easy to see why many parents faced with a non breakfast-eating child will be less fussy about the food they consume, reasoning that at least they're eating something. We let two of our children, Daniel and his step-sister Alex, go to school on a diet of Pop-Tarts (basically jam-filled pastries you heat up in the toaster) for months because we were just so glad they were eating something.

In the end we settled on toasted sandwiches, smoothies and, if all else failed, a banana. I have yet to meet a child who doesn't like the taste and as a food they have a lot going for them. They have lots of carbohydrates for energy, are low in fat, and are potassium-rich, which is great for muscles. They also have some protein and iron.

Instead of throwing an Up&Go at your child on the way to school, swap it for a banana and a carton of milk, which will give protein, calcium, zinc, vitamins A and B, and iodine.

I'm very much a toast and a cup of tea girl at breakfast, and it gives me enough energy, even with a gym work out to see me through to lunch. Which is when I go outside to raid the chicken coop and find some delicious, bright yellow-yolked eggs.

My Findings

Nestlé Milo Oats

I see this as a great transition product to get children who may be used to a diet of high sugar processed breakfast cereal used to the taste and texture of oats which are a very healthy option for the reasons above. By the time they've gone through a packet of these, they might just like a bowl of real porridge with some fresh banana and honey mixed in which is a less sweet option than this product and better for them. It also means that your child sets off on a cold winter's morning with a warm breakfast in their stomach, which is a nice old-fashioned thing to do, and the effect of the oats on their memory and listening skills might be good too.

SUMMARY:
- Three teaspoons of sugar in every serving if made with milk, but with water only one and a half teaspoons.

- 20g of oats in every serve which is a great option for good nutrition, and oats have proven benefits for your child's memory and listening skills.
- A great transition food to get your child interested in eating porridge on a winter's morning.

Kellogg's Froot Loops

There is just something irresistible to children about food which comes in fun colours and Froot Loops certainly fulfils that expectation. It even has the sell line "a fun fuel for adventurous kids."

There is no doubting your kids will love this cereal and hoover it down. But why not teach your children that real food doesn't come in six fun, mostly artificial colours? Most children are quite happy to eat Weet-Bix which by comparison has only 0.8g of sugar per serve or 6.8g per serve with milk. It also uses wholegrains and has more fibre. Top it with some fresh fruit, like strawberries and peaches, and you have a great breakfast with plenty of natural colour.

And perhaps follow a rule for eating by the author of Food Rules, Michael Pollan, who says "Don't eat breakfast cereals that change the colour of the milk."

SUMMARY:
- Contains 38 per cent sugar.
- Has three artificial colours which are banned in other countries.
- Uses natural flavourings.

—my recipes—

Porridge

Porridge was considered an economical choice to fill hungry tummies in the old days, but what Nana didn't know is that it is has a low glycemic index or GI, which means it provides energy slowly over a long period to give sustained energy. Oats in porridge are anti-inflammatory and very good for anyone with digestive problems, as they form a gel-like substance in the gut which encourages beneficial bacteria. Oats are also high in soluble fibre which helps reduce cholesterol and are rich in B vitamins, calcium, iron, magnesium, phosphorous and potassium.

Making porridge is seen as a time-consuming activity but it needn't be. Nana would have used wholegrain oats, which take a little longer to cook, but we can use rolled oats, which take just a few minutes. In the old days they would often soak the oats overnight, so I have included this instruction in my very simple, very fast porridge recipe.

  1 cup rolled oats
  2 cups cold water

Mix together in a pot with a pinch of salt and leave overnight to extract the maximum nutrition out of the oats and save time in the morning. Simply pop the pot on the element and bring to the boil, cook for 1 minute and serve with yoghurt or milk, honey or brown sugar.

For extra goodness, omega-3 and fibre add 1 tbsp flax

seed (also known as linseed) to the porridge.

You can also use wholegrain oats which are simply oats which haven't been chopped up like the rolled oats, but you will need to cook for five minutes in the morning.

You can substitute the water for milk if you like a creamier porridge.

Time taken: 5 minutes.

Low-fat Low-sugar Toasted Muesli

I first shared this recipe in *Mother's Little Helper* and I've had rave reviews as it's very hard to find a toasted muesli which isn't laden with oil. In fact, the original version of this recipe had 1 ½ cups of oil and 1 cup of honey. But I've reduced that substantially and replaced it with apple juice, which works really well. You only need a little bit of this muesli to fill you up, and it contains really good nutrients such as Brazil nuts (one a day keeps you loaded with selenium) Goji berries (immune enhancers) and flax seed or linseed (great fibre and omega-3 sources). If you grind up the linseeds first, you get more nutrition out of them as they pass through your digestive system.

¼ cup olive oil

¼ cup liquid honey

2 cups good quality apple juice

1kg wholegrain oats

1 cup pumpkin seeds

1 cup sunflower seeds

1 cup sesame seeds

1 cup coarsely grated coconut

1 cup coarsely chopped Brazil nuts
  1 cup coarsely chopped almonds
  1 cup flaxseed (also known as linseed)
  2 tsp ginger powder
  2 tsp cinnamon powder

Mix the olive oil with the liquid honey and apple juice. Place rest of muesli ingredients in a bowl and coat with the liquid, rubbing it into the oats and nuts with your hands. Put it in a large roasting dish (I need two) and toast in a 100°C oven for 1 ½ hours, stirring frequently until golden brown. Store in airtight container and prepare to love it.

EXTRAS: Stir in 1 cup sultanas and 1 cup Goji berries. You can also use chopped dried apricots or dates if you like. You can buy Goji berries at health stores, supermarkets and Asian stores, where you might find them called wolfberries. They look like red sultanas.

Time taken: 2 hours.

Bircher Muesli

Some people prefer this sort of muesli, which is basically soaked and flavoured rolled oats that are left overnight and go all mushy and delicious by the morning. This was invented in 1900 by the Swiss physician Maximilian Bircher-Benner for patients in his hospital, where a diet rich in fresh fruit and vegetables was an essential part of therapy.

  1 cup rolled oats
  Juice of 1 orange
  ½ cup live unsweetened yoghurt
  ½ cup chopped almonds

1 apple grated (leave skin on)

½ cup fresh berries (optional)

¼ cup water

Mix all ingredients together and put in a bowl in the fridge when you go to bed. In the morning take out and eat. It tastes delicious. If you like it stickier and more gooey replace the water with more yoghurt.

Time taken: 5 minutes plus soaking time.

Smoothies

These have to be the easiest thing in the world to make, as long as you have the ingredients on hand. Buy up frozen fruit, like berries and strawberries, and always have a couple of bananas in the freezer as well. Here are a few of my favourite recipes for you to try out on yourself and your kids, but feel free to experiment. Yoghurt keeps it creamy and fruit gives it flavour and colour. And if you have someone who can't eat dairy, replace the milk or yoghurt with soy milk.

There is one rule — do not use ice cream for a breakfast smoothie. That's just cheating.

Weet-Bix Smoothie

(Courtesy www.weetbix.co.nz)

1 cup milk or soy milk

1 Weet-Bix

1 chopped banana

½ cup frozen berries

Oatie Smoothie

1 tbsp rolled oats
1 banana
1 tsp honey
½ cup yoghurt
½ cup milk

Berry Smoothie

½ cup frozen berries
½ cup milk
1 banana

Green Smoothie

Otherwise known as a cheeky way to get some vegetables into your kids.

1 banana
½ cup frozen berries
½ cup mango, sliced
a handful of spinach leaves
3 lettuce leaves
a sprig of parsley
1 tbsp honey

Strawberry Pineapple Smoothie

1 cup frozen strawberries
¾ cup milk
¾ cup pineapple juice
½ cup yoghurt
1 tbsp honey
1 tsp wheat germ (optional)

Sweet Truth

Cereals with 40 per cent sugar, as found by *Consumer* magazine:
Signature Range Honey Poppas
Kellogg's Frosties
Kellogg's Froot Loops
Pams Honey Snaps
Pams Coco Snaps
Home Brand Cocoa Puffs
Budget Cocoa Puffs

CONCLUSIONS:
- Don't blame your grandkids for wanting to eat stuff that is bad for them. It's the marketing.
- As journalist Michael Pollan says in his book *Food Rules*: "Don't eat breakfast cereals that change the colour of the milk."
- For your kids' cereal, aim for less than 15g sugar, less than 400mg sodium and 5g to 15g fibre per 100g.
- If your child won't eat breakfast, throw a banana and a carton of milk at them in the car.
- Studies show that kids who have a good breakfast perform better at school.

CHAPTER SIX

bread

crust me, you'll loaf it

Bread is one of the most wonderful things to eat. Hot out of the oven it is crisp on the outside and soft and moist on the inside as you take your first bite. But the best thing about hot bread is the smell. It's the universal scent of comfort and has the power to intoxicate humans and have them running to the kitchen from far and wide.

Unfortunately, bread has been getting a bad run lately, as people avoid it in an effort to lose weight.

"I'm not doing carbs," they say. "You just don't need them."

As I write this my husband only eats carbs for breakfast and lunch as he tries to lose some weight. I happen to love that weight because it represents the kilos left behind after he put on 14kg when he stopped smoking five years ago — the best gift he could give his long-suffering wife and children.

When I met him he was a tall, slim smoker's smoker on a pack a day, sometimes more. He was one of those people who could eat anything and never put on weight. And eat he did. Fish and chips for lunch, a couple of pies a day, bacon and eggs for breakfast, big gourmet dinners (he is a great cook).

Unfortunately for me, my eating habits joined his, and I put on weight just by being in a relationship with him — weight I still have to lose.

My neighbour recently lost 10kg, mainly by cycling for hours around the city, but he also said "cutting carbs helps".

Personally, I think the people cutting carbs by not eating gorgeous bread would be better off not drinking alcohol first. But no matter, too much bread can be the culprit and in my efforts to join the healthy and perhaps drop from a size 16 to a 14 I eat less bread than I used to.

Ironically, my carb avoider is also the person who bakes a fresh loaf of sourdough in our kitchen every day. (He eats two slices for lunch also.)

Foodies all want to be able to have a sourdough starter and bake sourdough but it is one of those things that can be very difficult to achieve.

Over the years I have attempted to make my own sourdough starter — there are very complex recipes and instructions all over the internet.

I wanted to create my own yeast, as they used to in the old days. The idea is that your starter grows using the bacteria in the air where you live. This is supposed to be very good for you in terms of synergy and harmony and being in tune with the universe — or at least your suburb. I don't really buy into that, but I like the idea of a living, breathing organism making my bread, rather than some dried-up yeast granules, produced in a factory.

None of my efforts was very successful and then a friend of mine popped a starter in the letterbox in an old yoghurt container.

"There's a sourdough starter in your letterbox," she messaged me on Facebook. "Not sure what you do with it, but I'm sure you'll work it out."

I wasn't exactly prepared to accept something of such magnificence and to my knowledge I had never mentioned to my friend that I particularly wanted one.

But as we all know sometimes the most unexpected gifts turn out to be the best ones of all, in this case an 18-year-old starter which was created from apples.

I retrieved the jar of what looked like flour paste, lifted the lid and had my first whiff of live yeast. It smells like vinegar and is quite pleasant really. With it came a real estate agent's flyer and on the back my friend had hastily scrawled "Feed with half a cup of flour every day. Tip out if you get too much."

"Okay, I thought. Guess I'll work it out."

To be honest, the starter wasn't bubbling or doing the things I thought it should be doing, so I found myself acting out an episode of *Animal Rescue* where I am an SPCA worker desperately trying to save a starving kitten.

"What is that goop sitting in the sun inside my favourite beanie?" asked Paul when he came home.

"It's my sourdough starter. Don't frighten it, it's very sick and cold."

"Can I at least have a look?"

"No you can't, I'll tell you when it's safe."

Miraculously, after a feed and a warm-up it started bubbling away quite happily. I know it sounds crazy but I do actually believe that you need to love and talk to your starter as well as feed it. Just a little tip there for anyone starting out.

We all gathered around it at dinner and had a smell and welcomed our new pet to the household. Which is exactly what it has become. Two years later it goes by the nickname of Starty and is mollycoddled not by me but my husband who has taken over its care. If we go away then it becomes the responsibility of our daughter Hannah, who keeps Starty in the fridge and feeds it once a week. Apparently Pearl caught her talking to it once, but I didn't follow up on that. I was just glad she was giving it some love.

My next problem was how to use it to make bread. The only recipes I could find online were so complicated that you could train to be an astronaut, fly to the moon and back and still only be half way through making a loaf.

So I decided to wing it. We had been using a very simple French recipe for making bread for some time and so I simply replaced the half teaspoon of dried yeast in the recipe with 1 ½ cups of Starty.

"Are you sure it will work?" asked Paul, whose secret to being such a great cook is that he's scrupulous about sticking to the exact amounts in a recipe. "Faffing about" as he calls it, usually ends in tears. I'm a big faffer when it comes to cooking.

"The thing about bread," I told him, "is that it's a creative, loving process. It's give and take, it's understanding each other. Watch and learn."

He went back to his computer, giving me the look he uses for moments like these. He puts his chin down and turns his dark brown eyes in my direction for a little longer than is necessary. Basically it means, "You are completely mad but I love you."

The dough rose when it was supposed to, smelled great and then I popped it into the oven. I fully expected it to be a failure but a good start and what would no doubt be a huge sourdough learning curve.

"I'll probably spend the next week perfecting the recipe, but I'll get there in the end," I yelled out confidently to Paul.

And then it was cooked. The most beautiful loaf of bread emerged from the oven and it tasted excellent.

The family was astonished. And so was I.

I tweaked the salt a bit and added some sugar to counter the sour taste a little and that is the recipe we use every day. When I say we, I mean Paul.

After a month of being the sourdough queen, I predictably got a bit bored. I do this with my new discoveries. To date, the only interest which has maintained my constant attention has been the hens, who still have their coop cleaned out once a week, greens delivered daily and are generally doted on by myself. Paul did once point out that the only reason that happened was that he has steadfastly refused to help out.

"I know that the day I offer to clean out the coop is the day you get bored and hand it all over to me. And that's just never going to happen."

Paul doesn't like the chickens very much.

So with the bread my everyday loaf turned into my every second day loaf which turned into my once a week loaf which was cause for great distress in my family.

"I'm a bit over it to be honest," I told Paul when he asked if I could please make some bread for tomorrow.

"I'll do it," he said. And so he did. Paul is a man who likes routines and so for the past two years his daily routine includes preparing the dough before he goes to bed and then putting it in the oven in the morning. He's an early riser so that means most days we have hot, steaming bread for breakfast.

The best thing about the bread we make is that it has precisely five ingredients: flour, water, live yeast, salt and sugar.

The bread available in the supermarkets has more stuff in it. We all know that white bread is bad for you and brown bread is good. Yet white bread is such a big part of the Kiwi diet because we wrap sausages in it, sprinkle hundreds and thousands on it to make fairy bread and roll it up to make cheese rolls. And white bread remains one of our top selling supermarket foods.

A survey of Wellington supermarket shoppers in 2004 found that the most popular products bought were full-fat milk, white bread, sugary soft drinks and butter. And a Ministry of Health nutritional survey of children in 2002 revealed that white bread was the most commonly eaten variety. Over in Britain, however, sales of white bread fell by 1 per cent in 2010 while sales of brown bread increased by 6 per cent, so perhaps we are just late brown bread adopters.

The most popular brown bread in this country is Vogel's, which is missed by expats all over the world and has been produced in New Zealand for many years. The website informs us that the original mixed grain bread is baked to Swiss nutritionist Alfred Vogel's original 1950s recipe.

I found that Vogel's had seven ingredients, including added gluten, which is common in wholegrain breads to help the heavy dough rise, and skim milk powder. The white bread had nine ingredients, which included three emulsifiers, one acidity regulator and canola oil.

Both included iodised salt, which has been added to our commercially prepared bread since September 2009, when a number of studies revealed that the iodine levels were declining among New Zealanders. Iodine is an essential nutrient for humans and is only required in small amounts. One of the serious health effects of iodine deficiency disorders is goitre (enlargement of the thyroid gland, leading to a swelling of the neck). In very severe iodine deficiency, stunted growth and mental retardation can occur in children. Because of high rainfall and glaciations in this country, our soil is deficient in iodine, so plants grown here have low iodine levels, as do the animals which eat the plants. Table salt was iodised in 1924, and then the level was increased in 1938 along with a major public education campaign to ensure people understood the benefits of using iodised salt in the home.

The re-emergence of iodine deficiency appears to be due to New Zealanders eating more commercially prepared foods made without iodised salt, and people using less salt in their food at home in response to health messages to reduce salt intake.

In my home, we use salt in the most natural form we can find, which usually means it still has the iodine and minerals which are stripped out during the production of pure white table salt. My favourite is Himalayan rock salt which is a pink colour and has good levels of iodine, selenium and zinc. If you're not going to use a natural salt, then it is important that you use iodised salt in your food.

As I write this, there is debate about whether folic acid should be added to our bread. Pregnant women need adequate folic acid for the formation of DNA and other reproduction functions. If a woman doesn't get enough her child could be born with spina bifida, which is Latin for "split spine". It can cause leg weakness, paralysis and other severe problems.

Folic acid can be found in green vegetables, especially spinach, legumes, cashews, hazelnuts and almonds, corn and wheatgerm.

I'm not a great supporter of medicating the masses, because at the core of the work I do writing about the importance of real food and rejecting additive-laden processed foods, is freedom of choice. We already have a nation of people blindly eating additives in processed food. How do we know what the long-term effects will be of extra folic acid on people who don't need it? And the reason there is a deficiency of folic acid emerging is surely because as a nation we are eating fewer green vegetables, nuts and legumes in our diet, favouring instead nutritionally empty fast food and processed food.

I find it difficult to get my head around the fact that to make the white flour used in most of our bread, dozens of essential nutrients are removed or destroyed. So then we add them back or fortify it with vitamins and minerals.

I also know that every woman who gets pregnant and visits her GP is immediately given a prescription for folic acid so why does it need to go in our bread as well?

MAKING YOUR OWN bread is still seen as an impossibility for many people and I understand why. Both Paul and I work from home, so there is time to set it to rise, and then pop it in the oven and check on it. But the time spent actually making it is about 10 minutes all up, which isn't much to ask of even the busiest person in the world.

If you were really keen, you could bake it in the morning before you go to work, or when you get home from work, and incorporate hot, fresh bread in your dinner plans (unless of course, like everyone around me, you are avoiding carbs).

For most people being a weekend bread maker can be just the ticket. You can make a loaf for friends who are coming over for brunch, or just to impress your kids. I like to make pita bread for dinner some nights. It tastes nothing like the dried up things you get at the supermarket and kids love filling the bread with salad and chilli beans or meat and cheese. I also secretly like watching as the breads rise up and form pockets in the oven as I marvel at the science of food.

A good way to start making bread is to make pizza bread, which really is very easy and guaranteed to impress your family, served just as a bread slathered in olive oil and the herbed salt from Chapter One. Or rolled out thin as a base for pizza. Have a go at this one and then tell me you aren't hooked on bread making. The secret is that once you've got the hang of yeast, it becomes a joy, not a job.

Quite recently I began making crumpets after I tested them for my *New Zealand Woman's Weekly* "Nana's Pantry" column, where I seek out old recipes and reintroduce them to readers.

There is nothing quite like a hot homemade crumpet, drizzled with butter and perhaps a little honey, to make you feel all warm and cosy inside. Nana would have been very accomplished at making these, especially if, like mine, she came from Britain where these wonderful yeasty, doughy mounds were invented.

The holes in the top are created by adding baking soda to a yeast mix, and it is these very holes which allow the crumpet to soak up anything you choose to spread on it.

You can buy special crumpet rings in kitchen specialty shops — I even found non-stick ones — or keep an eye out in op shops, where I've often seen them going for a song. If you eat a lot of pineapple or beetroot from those small 5cm high cans you can wash the cans and take the bottom out of them to create perfect crumpet rings.

When I made these I thought it would take a few times to get it right. But the very first one popped out of the mould and revealed itself to be perfectly doughy and full of little holes ready to soak up the butter.

"Paul come and look at this," I shouted enthusiastically.

He walked into the kitchen and despite his no-carbs eating plan immediately picked that first perfect crumpet up and bit into it.

"Wait, I need a picture," I said and got out my iPhone to capture the moment.

After I posted it on Facebook one of Auckland's most renowned chefs, Tony Astle, who owns our oldest fine-dining restaurant, Antoine's, commented: "It looks like a bought one. You must have been practising a lot. Well done!!"

I felt very proud of myself and then the family came from far and wide to assemble in my kitchen, keen to accept a crumpet or two. And when they had run out I was requested to make another batch — immediately.

WHILE I'M WRITING this, I am sitting at a window looking out at the Waitemata Harbour from Mt Victoria in Devonport. Every time I write a book I reach a stage where I need to leave home. At home I can quite happily write my columns and newsletter around what is a working household. Downstairs we have all the Wendyl's Green Goddess products being made and sent out. Upstairs we have Paul and me in our offices typing out words. We also have two gorgeous grand-daughters who visit once a week, Pearl who at 14 still needs love and attention, frequent and very welcome visits from our adult children and partners, and then there is the menagerie of cats, dog and five hens.

"She never gets any time to herself," said a friend once, describing to someone what my life was like while I sat and listened. "I could never live your life," she said with the dread more commonly used for conversations discussing a cancer diagnosis.

At first I was a bit taken aback and a little angry at her perception of my life. At the time we did have five children living with us and it was true that there wasn't a lot of "me" time but I didn't like hearing it.

Then I had a wake-up call and realised that if I was going to write books I needed to escape the madness of home occasionally so that I could get into a long piece of writing without having to come out of it, as if from a dream, to tell someone where the scissors were, what the funny-looking thing on the kitchen table was, and when dinner is and what it is.

My first solo writing stint happened in Venice, where I went on a whim for two weeks. I adore Venice and at the time was writing a romance thriller set there. I imagined myself wandering the canals and tapping away on my laptop for hours pausing only to cater to my needs, not anyone else's.

But as news of my trip spread the reaction was overwhelmingly negative. One person close to me inquired if they had ashrams in Venice, dropping a huge dollop of suggestion that I might be having a mid-life crisis. Another person wondered why I would even consider travelling anywhere on my own when I had a nice husband to go with me, and suggested Hawaii would make more sense. I'm not sure why Hawaii. Perhaps a woman alone is better off wearing a coconut bra?

A colleague, live on the radio, stated that he was worried about my family. The inference surely being that when the woman of the house was away the children starved, the power was cut off and the Ebola virus moved in.

And then there were just the looks. From various people searching my face for signs of a marriage break-up, a terminal illness prompting me to get out my list of 100 things to do before I die, or an assignation with a lover of indeterminate nationality, but most probably Italian.

"No, seriously, I just want some time alone to write my novel which is set in Venice," I repeated until I was blue in the face.

Which then prompted a thought bubble above their heads which said: "She's taking herself a bit seriously isn't she?"

The only people who were quite happy for me to disappear were Paul and our five children. The very people I was escaping from with their love of interruption, need for nurture and givers of conversations I never regret finding time for.

And so I went to Venice where I shopped in my local village buying fresh fruit and vegetables from the man in a boat in the canal at the bottom of my street. I feasted on fresh asparagus lightly steamed in my apartment, ate tripe cooked in a wonderful tomato based sauce in the restaurant on the corner and had my hand slapped by an old Venetian woman who told me in no uncertain terms to stop squeezing the fruit. Even in her staccato Italian I got the message loud and clear.

In Venice there is no need to touch the fruit because it is all as fresh as you can get!

I also fell in love with the fresh anchovies they kept in oil, courgette flowers stuffed with cheese and fried, and delicious gorgonzola cheese, runny and eager to escape the paper it was wrapped in when I bought it home.

But I got incredibly lonely and wracked up a few hundred dollars in phone calls home to Paul. I nearly finished the novel, but then found once I was home it just stayed on my computer untouched.

One day I picked up the phone and rang the Michael King Writer's Centre for help. Writers are so lucky to have this place, which was set up after the death of one of our best writers, Michael King. It operates out of the old signalman's house on Mt Victoria. It's a lovely old cottage which has been cleaned up and serious writers — poets, playwrights, things like that — can do residencies in the bedroom and studio out the back for several months. Fortunately for me, they hire out the room in the front too, which is where I'm sitting now, for a very reasonable price, and this is where I sat five years ago and finished my novel.

It was the most intense two weeks of work I had ever achieved and every night I could drive back over the bridge to my family, or stay the night if it was going very well.

In between times I wrote my other books, *Domestic Goddess on a Budget* and *A Home Companion* down at my caravan, until that too became a little crowded.

The caravan used to be a "writer's dream" but that description eventually got replaced by "drop-in centre".

My last attempt to write at the caravan lasted four days and I didn't write a word. I was too busy attending to a stream of visitors.

"Are you there?" yelled the man who would turn out to be my final visitor.

It was too late to lie down on the lino and pretend I wasn't there, and besides Shirl was barking at him.

"Yes I am but I Am Very Busy Writing a Book!" I said as I peered out the front door.

He was clutching a weed. He informed me that it could be used to feed monarch butterflies. Apparently I had been talking about that on the radio the other day. I hadn't.

"Interesting," I said. "Thank you so much for that, now I really must get on."

"I've got a goat," he said resistant to my efforts to disappear.

"Lovely," I said.

"Would you like to come and milk it?"

This was a first for the visitors to the caravan. Over the years, I have been asked next door to drink two cocktails made with home-made spirits, with the result that I had to crawl home. I've been invited to go fishing and I've been called a sissy for not doing shots of something green and evil looking. But never have I been asked to do a bit of milking. And for a moment I was tempted. But then the book kicked in.

"Look, any other time, I'm just a bit busy."

"You could make cheese with it. I know you make a bit of cheese now and then."

"Yes I do, but not today. Thanks so much for the kind offer but I really must go. Cheerio."

The man left, still clutching the weed in his hand which he glared at as if it was to blame for my unwillingness to join him in some milking, then threw it down the bank.

So it was back to the Michael King Writer's Centre where I finished my last book *Mother's Little Helper* — another intense two weeks, and now I am here finishing this book.

The reason I am telling you this is because out the back when I arrived was a woman writing a play about breadmaking, in particular rewena, which is a traditional Maori bread. It also uses a bug or starter, just like sourdough.

I noticed her rewena bug in the fridge when I got here, but our paths only crossed for two days and we really only exchanged a few "hellos" and polite words.

When she left, a rewena bug stayed behind with instructions to Karren who runs the centre to give it to anyone who would like it.

I leapt on it with great enthusiasm when Karren offered it to me and now I'm learning the art of rewena which is yet another great gift the centre has given me.

By the way, the Venice romance thriller is still sitting stubbornly in my computer and refusing to come out to be published. It may have something to do with that fact that I have supreme confidence in myself to write non-fiction, but when it comes to fiction I'm a big sissy and not at all keen to have it criticised.

"One day," I tell myself. "When I've got nothing better to do."

Which is the same as saying "never".

My Findings: Bread

Vogel's Original Mixed Grain Vs Tip Top Super Soft White Sandwich

There are rumours that the brown colour of Vogel's is achieved by adding colours to the mix, but this is not so with this bread, which has no added colours, sugars or preservatives.

The lack of preservatives means you must keep it in the fridge if the weather is hot or humid.

It also has a low GI of 41, which means it takes longer to digest and therefore gives you a more even level of energy rather than a sharp spike.

The addition of whole grains wheat and rye into Vogel's, at 24 per cent per serve, means that for every two slices of this bread you get about 17g of wholegrains. There is no official recommended intake for wholegrains in our diet, but an independent industry group called Go Grains Health and Nutrition, which has members such as Sanitarium and Kellogg's, recommends each person eats 48g a day, so if you eat five and a half slices of Vogel's, you'll hit that target.

There is substantial evidence that wholegrains can help reduce the risk of heart disease and diabetes, help with weight management and assist in preventing some cancers — particularly colon cancer. So wholegrains are a good choice in your diet. These wholegrains also give the bread 2.9g of fibre per two slices. The wholegrains also give you added nutrition, particularly folic acid, magnesium, and vitamin E.

When it comes to nutrition, it is hard to look past Vogel's, as it has more protein at 6.4g per serve than Tip Top at 4.9g. More fibre at 2.9g per serve than Tip Top at 1.5g. And, because of the wholegrains in Vogel's, you are also getting extra nutrition and a much lower GI.

The addition of the oil in Tip Top means it is higher in fat at 1.2g per serve where Vogel's is 0.7g. So your first choice should be Vogel's even though you can wash the dishes and dry them in the time it takes to toast it. If your family really insists on white bread though, Tip Top does one called Oatilicious which has added oats and therefore fibre without affecting the texture of the bread.

SUMMARY
- Contrary to some rumours Vogel's does not use colouring to give their bread a brown colour. It has no added sugars, preservatives or artificial ingredients.
- Tip Top Super Soft has four added ingredients to emulsify and regulate pH as well as oil.
- To match Vogel's wholegrain and fibre content upgrade your white bread to one with added oats.

— *my recipes* —

Easy White Bread

This is a very simple recipe which anyone can master and the result is a beautifully crisp loaf you can be proud of. Although this is a white bread it has no added fats or sugars, which many homemade breads do. And you can make a wholemeal version easily by substituting one cup of the white flour for wholemeal flour. You can use ordinary high-grade flour from your supermarket, but like anything, the better quality your ingredients the more nutritious the food. So if you can source stoneground flour, go for it.

    3 cups white flour (for wholemeal use 1 cup

wholemeal flour and 2 cups white flour)
¼ tsp granulated yeast
1 ¼ tsp salt
1 ½ to 2 ½ cups of water

Mix the flour, yeast and salt in a bowl. Pour the water in slowly and stir until you have a sticky — not stiff — dough. Sometimes I need just 1 ½ cups of water, at others I need the full 2 ½ — it depends on the flour you use and the climate. If you get a sloppy dough, don't worry, it will still make great bread, it'll just be a nightmare to work with. Cover with a tea towel and let it prove (rise) in a warm place for 12 to 24 hours. I leave mine by the fire when I go to bed in the winter, or you could put it in a hot water cupboard or on top of your fridge.

The dough is ready to use when you lift the tea towel and see the surface is dotted with bubbles. Don't be alarmed if it looks like a sloppy batter; this is the way it should look. Get lots of flour and sprinkle it on a work surface so that you have a thick covering. You don't want to see any surface through the layer of flour. Tip the bread dough out onto the surface, sprinkle the top with lots more flour and fold it over on itself a few times so that it is a mound, and then cover with a tea towel and leave for 15 minutes to recover. Do not be surprised if it starts expanding and creeping out onto the work surface during this time.

Flour your hands generously and shape the dough into a ball. Coat a tea-towel liberally with flour — again, you want a really thick covering — and then put the ball of dough onto the tea towel and wrap loosely. Leave in a warm place for two hours so that it can double in size.

Half an hour before the dough is ready, put a 2-litre

casserole pot or Dutch oven — I use a heavy cast-iron pot with lid — into a hot oven at 230°C to heat up. When the dough is ready, take the pot out of the oven, put the bread into it and give it a shake to settle it into the pot. Place back in the oven with its lid on for 20 minutes, and then cook without the lid for the next 10 minutes, until the loaf is nicely brown on top. Remove from the oven, inhale and enjoy.

Time taken: 40 minutes plus proving time.

Sourdough Bread

This uses the same process as above but we have made some slight alterations to the ingredients and the cooking times. Like the plain bread, you can also add some wholemeal flour if you like.

3 cups flour
2 tsp sugar
1 tsp salt
1 ½ cups starter

Mix the flour, starter, sugar and salt in a bowl. Pour the water in slowly and stir until you have a sticky — not stiff — dough. Follow directions for Easy White Bread, but when it comes to baking cook for 35 minutes covered and then 6-7 minutes uncovered to brown.

Time taken: 40 minutes plus proving time.

Pita Bread

2 tsp sugar
1 cup lukewarm water

2 tsp dried yeast granules
3 cups flour
1 tsp salt

Combine sugar and warm water then sprinkle over the yeast. Set aside in a warm place and wait until it froths and smells "yeasty" (about 10 minutes).

Put the flour in a big bowl and fluff up with a whisk while you are waiting for the yeast to bubble.

Pour the yeast mixture into the flour and mix to a dough, you might need to add more flour or more water to get an easy to work with consistency.

Knead the dough for 10 minutes, then put back in the bowl and cover with a tea towel. Put in a warm place until the dough has risen and doubled in size (usually about an hour).

Sprinkle the salt over the dough and knead again for five minutes. Then divide the dough into between 8 and 12 pieces, depending on how big you want your pita bread to be. Roll them out into circle shapes but not too thin — about 10mm is right.

Place each pita bread on some baking paper and leave to rise for another hour while you heat up the oven to 200°C, with a baking tray inside to get hot.

To cook, slide the pita bread dough onto the hot baking tray one or two circles at a time.(I use my small nana oven for this.)

Watch them carefully as they puff up in about two or three minutes, and when they are light gold in colour, remove them from the oven and cook the rest.

Time taken: 30 minutes plus proving time.

Pizza Bread

This is such a staple — and so popular — I've put it in every book I've written (apart from the unpublished novel, although who knows?).

>2 tsp active granulated yeast (not Surebake)
>½ tsp sugar
>1 ½ cups of warm water
>4 large cups of high grade flour
>salt and pepper
>1 cup of chopped basil or parsley (optional)
>4 tbsp olive oil
>extra flour (if required)

Put yeast and sugar into warm water and mix together. Set aside in a warm place. Sift flour with salt and pepper into a bowl and add basil or parsley if you like. It is just as good without the herbs. When the yeast mixture starts to froth — and only when it froths — mix in olive oil. Add the yeast mixture to the flour and mix to a dough. Add more flour if it's a little sticky. Don't knead. Put in bowl in warm place and leave to rise for about an hour or until doubled in size. (If you can't find a warm place for the dough to rise, which can be hard in winter, simply fill a hot-water bottle and sit the bowl on that.) Pat out into breads and barbecue or fry. Brush with olive oil and sprinkle with lots of sea salt.

>Time taken: 10 minutes plus proving time.

Billy Bread

This is a really traditional Kiwi bread to make when camping.

>3 cups flour
>3 tsp baking powder

1 tbsp golden syrup
Enough milk to mix

Mix all ingredients in a large bowl, adding enough milk to make a dough. Place in a greased, closed tin or billy. You can then place this in embers of a beach fire or barbeque, covering the tin with coals for about half an hour (depending on the heat of your coals). Or you can cook it in a conventional oven in a cake tin at 190°C for about half an hour.

Another old cookbook of mine says to roll bits of the dough around sticks and then hold them over the fire, turning so that you get little buns on the end of the sticks. You can then fill the holes left by the sticks with butter, jam or cheese.

Time taken: 40 minutes.

Best Wholemeal Bread

Sometimes you just want to make a really healthy, stodgy, wholegrain bread. All my early efforts resulted in a loaf as heavy and thick as a brick, which wasn't at all appetising. This is the best recipe I've found for a loaf which combines wholegrains with height. When buying kibbled grain, you can get kibbled wheat, kibbled spelt — whatever you can find.

1 ½ cups kibbled whole grain (I buy this at supermarkets in their bulk food bins)
600ml whole milk, heated
2 tbsp olive oil
4 tbsp honey
3 cups white flour

3 cups wholemeal flour (use stone-ground if you can find it)

1 cup gluten flour

1 tsp salt

2 8g sachets of granulated yeast

Wash the grain in hot water and then put in a bowl and cover with 500ml of the hot milk. Add oil and honey. Stir to combine and leave to cool.

Leaving the remaining 100ml of milk to cool to lukewarm, then add yeast and 1 tsp of extra honey. Leave for 10 minutes until it is frothy.

Sift flours and salt together.

Mix the yeast in with the grain and stir. Then add enough flour to make a very sticky dough with a similar consistency to porridge.

Allow to rise for half an hour, covered, in a warm place. Add enough of the remaining flour to make a good soft dough which you can knead. You may need to add more flour than allowed in the recipe.

Knead for 10 minutes and then shape into two loaves which you put into two greased loaf tins. Bake at 200°C for 30 minutes, or until it sounds hollow inside when you tap the top gently.

Time taken: 1 hour plus proving time.

Crumpets

Yeast mixture

125ml milk

125ml water

2 tsp dried yeast (not Surebake)*

2 tsp caster sugar

Flour mixture
>1 ½ cups flour
>½ tsp salt

Baking soda mixture
>125ml warm water
>½ tsp baking soda

For the yeast mixture, gently warm the milk and water until it is room temperature. Do not make this too hot or you will kill your yeast. Test it as you would milk in a baby's bottle -it should just feel warm to the touch. Stir in the sugar until dissolved, and then sprinkle the yeast over the top, gently mixing in. Leave in a warm place for about 10 minutes until it starts to bubble and has a very yeasty smell.

In a bowl, combine the flour and salt and give it a good stir with a whisk to fluff it up. When the yeast is ready, make a well in the centre and add the yeast mixture, mixing until you have a dough. Cover with a tea towel and set in a warm place to rise for about an hour, or until it has doubled in size — whichever comes sooner.

Combine the baking soda and the water — again just blood temperature, not too hot. Stir this into the dough gently. You will find that the dough really doesn't want to accept the baking soda mixture but keep at it until it is mixed together and has formed a thick batter. Cover with a tea towel and leave to rest for 30 minutes.

Get a large frying pan or a griddle and grease it with oil or butter. Also grease your crumpet rings. Use a medium to low heat and place the rings on the pan. Pour enough batter into each so that it comes up just 1 cm on the rings. Don't fill the rings or you will get huge crumpets. Cook gently until bubbles appear and pop on top, then take the ring off and flip over to cook the bubbled side for just a minute or so until it is golden.

Put on a wire rack and serve while hot with lashings of butter. You can also add honey, jam or golden syrup. Some people even like Marmite.

Time Taken: 20 minutes.

*When buying dried yeast, Edmonds produce boxes which have 12 little sachets in them. I think this keeps the yeast fresher and each sachet has enough in it for most recipes.

Conclusions
- Making bread is one of the easiest ways to connect with the Nana inside you. Every day millions of people all over the world make bread.
- Commercial bread can contain additives you don't need. All commercial bread is fortified with iodine, and there are moves to add folate as well.
- Once you get into the habit of making bread, it no longer seems like the difficult exercise it once did.

Chapter Seven

meal solutions

when the answer is a problem

"Analyse 68-ingredient frozen pizza" reads a mention in my diary from two years ago.

I had just started the food column and a reader emailed me with a request to look into it.

I bought it at the supermarket the next week, took a quick look at it, uttered an expletive and placed it firmly in the freezer.

I had done a quick count standing there in front of my fridge and found that in the tiny print on the ingredients panel were 68 items.

"All that for one pizza," I mumbled to myself, vowing to get it out and have a look at it for my very next column.

When my very next column deadline came around I just couldn't face it. With all those ingredients I'd have to spend days on it.

"Maybe next week."

And so the pizza stayed safe from my prying eyes in the freezer for months on end as I procrastinated my way out of looking at it week after week.

Or so I thought.

About six months later I finally got up the energy and the time to have a crack at it, only to find that it had disappeared.

"Who ate the 68-ingredient pizza?" I asked the family that night at dinner.

"We did," answered Pearl. "Ages ago. It was really good."

I rolled my eyes.

"Really? All 68 ingredients were really satisfying and enjoyable? Every single one of them?"

"Yup," she said.

"And you, Daniel, what have you to say for yourself?"

As Pearl's older brother, Daniel is often complicit in late-night eating sprees thought up by his younger sister. Mainly because he finds it hard to say no to her and also because he's a big kid inside a 26-year-old's body.

So, I bought another one and placed it firmly in the freezer.

This one got eaten one night when we were out and Daniel was babysitting.

In the end, my procrastination and my children's hunger combined to ensure that five 68-ingredient pizzas were bought, frozen, cooked and devoured without ever seeing an analysis in my column.

When I started writing this book, I planned each chapter out in my notebook and wrote those fateful words again under this chapter heading.

"Analyse 68-ingredient frozen pizza." Only this time I added five!!!!! after the word "pizza" and then a simple instruction: "Go on, just bloody do it."

It may not surprise you to learn that this was the last chapter I wrote, such was the power to put off the 68-ingredient pizza.

And when I finally got around to it, I was relieved to find that it wasn't nearly as scary as I thought it would be, although it still took an awfully long time.

For a start, quite a few of the ingredients were repeated on the ingredients list. Water, salt and sugar appeared three times for instance and 10 other ingredients appeared twice.

So I recalculated and found that it only had 51 ingredients.

"Only 51," I said to myself. "You say that like it's okay to make a pizza with 51 ingredients."

Which of course it's not. I also found that one of the ingredients, "barbeque sauce" — which if you make it yourself has 12 ingredients — did not have its ingredients listed, because it makes up only 2 per cent of the total product and therefore the producer is not obliged to list them.

According to our Food Standards you "don't have to include the sub-ingredients of a compound ingredient in the ingredients list" if it is less than 5 per cent.

"But technically, if you add those onto the 51, you've got 63," I said to Paul when I got home that night.

"So what is it? 68, 51 or 63?" he said, no doubt wishing the pizza procrastination party would come to an end.

"I'll leave it at 51."

By now you are probably wondering how it takes

even 51 ingredients to make a pizza which, if you made it at home, would take a bit of cheese, some smoked chicken, a bit of bacon, some tomato and a pizza base. That's five ingredients. And that's where I would have to point out that to make a piece of smoked chicken you buy at the supermarket takes 19 ingredients, bacon takes 22, cheese takes five and tomato sauce takes seven. Your pizza base, even if you make it yourself, takes five, so technically you are making a pizza with 58 ingredients. And once you take into account the double-up ingredients you can bring it down to 41 but that's still a lot.

Enough to put you off pizza?

My analysis of The Chicago Pizza Company's BBQ Chicken and Bacon Gourmet Pizza found that the pizza had 21 natural ingredients such as flour, water, salt, sugar, milk, rennet, pork and chicken, and 25 additives, five of which are a concern for healthy eaters like myself.

So buying a frozen pizza is a great way to incorporate a lot of unnecessary additives into your family's diet, mainly because of the preservatives, colourings and flavourings added to the meat.

To make a low-ingredient pizza you can opt instead for sliced cooked chicken, beef or lamb (see Chapter One) instead of processed meats and cut out most of the additives. Make your own pizza base (see Chapter Six) and instead of using a commercially prepared tomato sauce go without and use sliced tomatoes and heaps of cheese and herbs. Ingredient count? A mere 12 if you use one meat, 13 if you use two.

I'VE CALLED THIS chapter "meal solutions" because I've always found the term quite funny when I see it in supermarket aisles. It implies that a meal is a puzzle or something confusing which necessitates a hunt for a long sought-after solution. Which, if you're in the "meal solutions" aisle, is usually a packet of chemicals and additives that you add to real food, or a ready-made meal in a packet to which you simply add water.

One thing you'll always find in that aisle is instant noodles. I looked into a brand which was frequently on sale at a very good price in my supermarket. I bought them as a "meal solution" for Pearl, who loved them and would get through 10 of these in a week if I let her.

Instant noodles are every parent's friend. Most school age kids love the taste and can cook them themselves in a few minutes. Unfortunately, they are high in carbohydrates, saturated fat and salt, and low in fibre, vitamins and minerals.

What I found on closer examination was a snack which takes moments to prepare but needs 38 ingredients and additives to achieve the spicy, meaty and salty taste. My daughter was basically eating some noodles soaked in a chemical soup which had very little real food in it.

We've never had them in the house since, much to Pearl's regret, and recently I was shocked to hear that a very health-conscious vegan friend of mine was basically living on them.

"He's just too busy to cook and it keeps him going," said his girlfriend. "And they do taste good."

"We'll see about that," I said, hurrying off to my laptop to pull up the 18-month-old column to email to him. And fortunately I could send him an alternative noodle recipe (see below), using plain noodles flavoured with soy sauce, which I invented in my desperation to wean my daughter off instant noodles.

After it was published in my column I went to stock up on plain unflavoured instant noodles at my local supermarket only to find they had sold out, which gave me a spring in my step. I naturally attributed this to unprecedented high demand prompted by my column rather than such implausible alternatives as the truck having broken down.

SOME PEOPLE JUST love a warming cup of soup for a meal solution, especially in winter. Soups are traditionally slow-cooked, highly nutritious dishes, containing the natural flavours and colours of meat and vegetables.

And up until 1949 that was the only soup you could get. But in that year the first dried soup was invented and in 1972 came the launch of Cup a Soup with the advertisement I can still sing in my head "Nobody makes. Soup in a cup. Like Continental Cup a Soup!"

My childhood was littered with little sachets which were treated in our home as easy lunches or just a hot drink if you needed one. The whole idea of the Cup a Soup marketing was that it was quick to prepare, especially at work, and you could wrap your hands around the mug and feel all warm and cosy. More recently an ad campaign in the UK showed a woman receiving a huge hug from two ape-like big furry blue arms while she drank the soup at her office. "A great big hug in a mug," was the catchline.

In the early days I'm sure sachets of instant soup did contain some real, dried ingredients, but that isn't what I found when I looked into a popular tomato soup designed for a cup. The soup looked bright red and creamy on the box and was 98.5 per cent fat free. But the amount of tomato in the rich tomato soup was 1 per cent or 0.78g which is just over a 10th of a teaspoon of tomato puree. Which means most of the ingredients in the packet were flavours, colourings, emulsifiers and preservatives (23, to be exact) including three colours which are banned in other countries.

So the wonderful nutritious soups that we used to eat a little more than 60 years ago have now been replaced by steaming hot mugs of chemicals with little nutritional value.

I encourage anyone to turn back the years, and if you're going to eat soup, make it one like your Nana would have made before mass production of food began following World War II.

This doesn't mean you have to make your own, it just means that you have to move down the supermarket aisle about two steps to the left or right and go for a canned soup. I found one which was 97 per cent fat free, had no preservatives, artificial colours or flavours and was 90 per cent tomatoes. It takes two minutes to heat up in a microwave and five minutes on a stove. I think that's time well spent if you're avoiding chemicals and eating real food. And you still get a quick, hot soup. And you can still wrap your hands around the mug and feel all warm and cosy, you just won't get a hug from some hairy blue ape arms.

And if you're feeling like ramping up your real food soup intake even more, you can go for one of the many fresh soups which are now appearing in supermarket refrigerators. Or why not make your own for the best nutrition option and freeze them in sealable plastic bags to take to work?

BEEF STOCK IS another one of those old-fashioned foods which not only used up bits of old bones, meat and vegetables, but became a flavour base for so many meals such as stews, soups and sauces. The good news is that bones cooked slowly are very nutritious. They are rich in minerals such as calcium, magnesium and zinc, which when released through long cooking are in a form easily absorbed by the body. The cartilage and tendons, when broken down, contain chondroitin and glucosamine, which are sold as supplements to ease arthritis and joint pain.

Instant stock powder has been accepted into most homes as a standby for adding a bit of flavour to casseroles or as a base for soup. Just dissolve 1 tsp of this product in a cup of hot water and you have a liquid which tastes like beef, but is it beef? In the old days invalids were fed broth, which is really a stock, while they were recuperating. I'm not sure you'd want to make up a cup of instant stock for an invalid, however, as the most disappointing finding from my analysis was that beef makes up only 1.5 per cent of the stock powder. This is a big surprise, as the main ingredient for a homemade beef stock would, of course, be beef bones.

I no longer have stock powders in my house, after discovering that the chicken stock powder had only 8 per cent chicken in it.

If I want some umami (meaty) flavour in something, I'll throw in a teaspoon of Our Mate, which is yeast extract. Or a dash of soy sauce often does the trick.

I also use stock gels, which have recently come on the market and contain far more nutrition, have 67 per cent chicken, and nine ingredients compared to 14 for stock powder and five for real stock.

Of course you can buy real stock in the supermarket, but it does get expensive at about $4.83 per litre, which means if you need enough to make a big pot of soup which holds five litres you are spending $24.15 on what is essentially a product of old bones and vegetables.

I do encourage you to have a go at making your own stocks. It can seem time consuming but actually most of the time is in the cooking, when you can be doing other things.

ONE OF THE cooking fads to come along during my childhood in the 1970s was putting your food in plastic bags before you placed it in the oven. It was advertised as a "no-mess" way to cook food, and it really appealed to my mother, who grasped the technology with enthusiasm.

I have to admit that, up until I looked at seasoned roasting bags for the column, I avoided them like the plague. The thought of heating up meat inside a plastic bag had me imagining all sorts of chemicals leaching from the bag into the food. A bit like when you used to buy a chicken and roast it, but forgot to take out the little plastic bag inside, in which they used to put the livers and kidneys. These were seen as valuable nutrition, and good chefs would cook them along with the chicken and include them in the gravy or in the stuffing. I often forgot and would have to reach in and pull out a melted mess which had given a plastic flavour to the whole bird.

But the good news is that I could find no evidence that cooking in the bag is harmful. The bags used are made out of a nylon which can withstand high heats. I've since used roasting bags to cook a very flavoursome turkey using herbs and spices, unlike the "meal base" I analysed. The Cook in Bag Honey BBQ Chicken contains a sachet of flavouring powder and an oven bag into which you pop some chicken drumsticks and the contents of the powder sachet before cooking.

What I discovered was that the flavouring powder was mostly sugar. For every 13g serve of this recipe base, there was a massive 11.3g of sugar, which is nearly three teaspoons. That means nearly 12 tsp in the whole flavouring sachet.

"So why don't you save yourself the 15 ingredients it takes to make this powder and just sprinkle some chicken legs with 12 teaspoons of sugar mixed with some spices and be done with it," I wrote in my column. "Or you could forgo the sugar and just cook the chicken legs sprinkled with a bit of salt and some herbs, or perhaps some soy sauce mixed with a little honey. And if you want to cook it in an oven bag, buy those separately."

The flavouring sachet also had artificial sweeteners in it, including cyclamate, which has been banned in the United States since 1970 because animal studies indicated that it caused cancer.

RICE RISOTTO WAS one of the first packaged meals to hit supermarket shelves during my childhood and gave busy homemakers an easy dinner to prepare. It was the ultimate "meal solution". You simply threw it all in a pot and came back 20 minutes later to find — hey presto — rice risotto.

When I looked at the ingredients list of a packet of Roast Beef Rice Risotto my eye went straight to "risone pasta", which is little bits of pasta in the shape of rice and I spent the afternoon fuming that there was no rice in my rice risotto. On later inspection I realised there was rice, but for some reason this product uses both.

Call me old-fashioned, but I quite like to know that when I'm eating something called Roast Beef Rice Risotto that it will have beef and rice. There was rice but also the pasta and a bunch of flavourings which are designed to make my tongue think I'm eating roast beef along with colouring.

I can see why this box would be appealing to

a busy mum eager to get a rice dish on the table in 20 minutes. But having looked at the instructions they are pretty much exactly the same as those for making a risotto from scratch. So here's an idea. Do that, and eliminate artificial flavours and colours in your family's next risotto meal.

My Findings: Meal Solutions

Not all "meal solutions" are bad for you. Over the years I have reviewed some outstanding examples of good food which is packaged and ready for busy people and I can recommend them to you:

MTR AluMethi (potato and fenugreek curry)

— No artificial colours, flavours or preservatives.
— All real food ingredients.
— Imported from India.

Bellisimo All Natural Chicken Arrabiata

— All real food, no artificial colours, flavours or preservatives.
— Reasonably low in fat.
— Manufacturer has signed up to industry standards to ensure quality of the product.

Naked Panda Green Chicken Curry with Noodles

— Has 21 ingredients, most of which are natural, real food.
— Has polysorbate60, which is known to cause cancer in animals and is mostly used in cosmetic products but levels in this product are quite low.
— Fat levels are okay at 10 per cent but sugar and salt are a little high.

Dolmio Pasta Bake — Tuna Bake Sauce

— Incorporating a can of tuna into this bake is a great way to get omega-3 fatty acids into growing children.
— It takes 18 ingredients to make what is essentially a cheese sauce that has four ingredients when home made.
— No artificial flavours or colours are in this product.

Deli-Menu Fish Pie with Tuna

— Only three additives in the can.
— The vegetables listed on the label can be found well represented in the can.
— Uses "dolphin friendly" tuna.

—my recipes—

Additive-free Noodles

    1 cake unflavoured noodles (Highmark Egg noodles fine cut are good)

Sauce

    ½ cup low salt soy sauce
    2 garlic cloves, crushed.
    2 tsp chilli sauce (sweet for kids, a little hotter for adults)
    ¼ tsp sesame oil

Make up the sauce by mixing the ingredients together and keep in a bottle in the fridge.

Cook the noodle cake per packet directions and then pour on 2 tbsp of the sauce mix. This will give you a quick snack which has five ingredients (although soy sauce has food acids and chilli sauce has a stabiliser).

Time taken: Five minutes for the sauce. Five minutes for the noodles.

Tomato Soup

    1 large onion, finely diced
    2 tbsp butter
    2 tbsp olive oil
    1 dozen ripe tomatoes or 3 cans whole tomatoes in juice
    5 tbsp tomato paste

⅓ cup flour

1 litre (about 4 cups) chicken or vegetable stock

1 tbsp sugar

1 cup cream

1 cup milk

Salt to taste

Basil, coriander or parsley to garnish

Sauté onion in butter and oil. Roughly cut tomatoes (I do this in a food processor) and add to pot. Cook for 10 minutes on a low heat, stirring occasionally. Add in tomato paste. Mix flour with same amount of stock in a small bowl until there are no lumps. Add to pot and stir in the rest of the stock slowly. Simmer for 30 minutes, stirring occasionally.

Remove from heat and blend in your blender, a few cupfuls at a time.

Return blended mix to a pot and heat. Add sugar, make sure mixture is not boiling before you add milk and cream. If it is too hot they will curdle. Taste mixture and add a little salt to taste.

Serve garnished with fresh herbs.

Time taken: 50 minutes.

Beef Stock

You can skip the roasting step in this recipe if you are in a hurry but I really recommend you take the time, as it adds a lot of flavour.

2 ½kg beef bones (ask your butcher to choose meaty ones for you for the best flavour)

2 large onions, chopped in half

2 carrots washed and unpeeled, chopped in half

2 celery stalks, cut into pieces
10 whole peppercorns.
3 cloves
3 garlic cloves (pop in whole and unpeeled)
Rosemary, thyme, parsley made into a little bouquet and tied with string
2 bay leaves, fresh or dried

Put the bones in a roasting pan and cook them for half an hour on 230°C. You want them to be nicely browned.

Meanwhile, in a little oil in a big stock pot, sauté the onions, carrots and celery until they look clear. Add the browned bones (making sure you scrape every bit of meaty, sticky goodness from the pan) and the rest of the ingredients.

Add enough water to cover the bones and vegetables (about 4 to 5 litres) and then bring to the boil. Gently simmer for five hours, skimming off any stuff which floats to the surface.

When it is ready it should taste delicious, but do not salt. You can salt it later, when you add it to your food. Strain and cool. Once it is cold you can skim off any fat before pouring into 1 litre containers and freezing.

Time taken: Five hours (unroasted). Five and a half hours.

Chicken Stock

You can buy chicken carcasses at butchers and some supermarkets or you can simply store carcasses left over from your roast chickens in the freezer and use them when you have enough.

5 or 6 chicken carcasses

1 onion chopped in half

1 carrot, unpeeled chopped in bits

1 leek, thickly sliced

1 celery stick chopped

A good bunch of parsley

1 bay leaf (fresh or dried)

10 peppercorns

Put all ingredients in a large stockpot and cover with water (about 5 to 6 litres).

Bring to the boil and simmer for 4 hours. Strain and let cool. Skim off any fat and then pour into containers to put in the freezer.

Time taken: Four hours.

Aromatic Turkey/Chicken in a Bag

This is a recipe from Julie Biuso which I clipped way back in 2000 and have had in my cookbook ever since. It is a foolproof way of making that Christmas turkey tender and moist and also a great way just to cook a chicken any old night.

1 small free-range turkey (about 3.3 to 5kg) or a very large free-range chicken

1 lime cut into eighths

4 stalks fresh lemon grass, bruised with a mallet

1 head of garlic, broken into cloves and bruised with a mallet

5cm section of fresh ginger, sliced

2 kaffir lime leaves

4 large coriander roots, bruised with a mallet

Olive oil

Salt and freshly ground black pepper

Rinse the cavities of the bird (turkey or chicken) and pat dry with paper towels. Remove any lumps of fat from inside the cavities. Stuff the main cavity with all of the ingredients except for the oil and seasoning. Close the cavity with a skewer or stitch the skin together. Tie the legs together with string. Rub the skin with plenty of olive oil and season well with salt and pepper.

Put the bird into an oven bag and put it in a roasting dish. Don't secure the bag tightly, just tuck the ends in loosely under the turkey — ignore any instructions that tell you to do otherwise.

Place the bird in a 200°C oven (regular not fan bake) and cook for approximately two hours. A 3.3kg turkey will take about 1 hour and 45 minutes.

Roasting turkey or chicken in the oven this way produces lots of delicious juices which can be skimmed of fat, extended with a little stock and bubbled up to make a gravy.

Once the bird is well rested, carve and serve.

Time taken: Two hours

Risotto

2 tbsp olive oil

1 onion, chopped

1⅛ cups arborio rice

1 litre chicken stock, hot

25g butter

⅓ cup grated parmesan cheese

Salt and freshly ground black pepper

Heat the oil in a large, heavy-based pan or casserole dish. Add the onion and cook for 5 minutes, until soft and translucent. Add rice, coat in oil, and cook for 2 minutes. Add the stock, a ladleful at a time. Keep stirring until most of the stock has been absorbed before adding the next ladleful. When all the stock has been absorbed and your rice is plump and creamy, stir in butter and parmesan. Add salt and pepper to taste.

Time taken: 20 minutes.

What Shall We Have for Saturday's Tea?

I found this chapter heading in one of my old cookbooks and it reminded me of the days when Saturday tea (or dinner) was a very slight affair. In Nana's day the traditional roast was planned for Sunday lunch after church, so Saturday night was regarded as a simple meal which usually revolved around toast and things made with cheese, tinned corn or eggs.

Welsh Rarebit, Curried Eggs and Scalloped Sweetcorn were often served up for a light tea before everyone settled down to the wireless and a spot of knitting.

These days, Saturday night dinners tend to take on monumental proportions as we entertain our friends over three-course meals made from recipes clipped from foodporn magazines because only at the weekends do we have time to stretch our fine cuisine cooking.

I think these three simple Saturday teas should make a comeback for quick meal solutions to serve the kids before leaving them to the babysitter on a Saturday night or for a light Sunday night meal after a big weekend. And if, like me, you have vegetarians in the house, these will all fit the bill nicely.

Welsh Rarebit

This dish was originally called Welsh Rabbit but then over the years got changed to Welsh Rarebit. The name was first used in 1785 and is thought either to be a reference to the fact that rabbit was the poor man's meat in England while in Wales cheese was the poor man's rabbit, or to be a slur on the Welsh, implying that if they went hunting for rabbits all they would have to eat at the end of the day would be cheese!

    4 slices toast
    250g cheddar cheese grated
    25g butter
    1 egg, lightly beaten
    1 tsp mustard
    1 tbsp Worcestershire sauce
    2 tbsp milk or cream
    Pinch of cayenne pepper

Toast the bread and butter it. Put the rest of the ingredients in a saucepan and heat gently, stirring until it thickens. Spread on toast and finish under a hot grill.

    (My father used to add chopped boiled eggs which makes a nice addition.)

    Time taken: 15 minutes.

Curried Eggs

- 4 hard-boiled eggs cut lengthwise into quarters
- 2 tsp curry powder
- 40g butter
- 1 onion finely chopped
- 1 tbsp flour
- ¾ cup milk
- A squeeze of lemon juice
- 1 tbsp finely chopped parsley

Melt the butter and sauté the onion, but do not brown. When onion is clear sprinkle on the flour and curry powder and cook for a few minutes to release the spices. Slowly stir in the milk and cook on a medium heat until the sauce thickens. Squeeze in a little lemon juice. Add the boiled eggs and chopped parsley plus pepper and salt to taste. When heated through, serve on hot buttered toast.

Time taken: 10 minutes, plus another 10 if you need to boil the eggs.

Scalloped Sweet Corn

This recipe was sent in to the *Cookery Book of the Ever Ready Committee of the Victoria League* in 1950 by Mrs L.S. Rickerby of Mt Eden.

- 1 tin creamed sweetcorn
- 1 egg
- 2/3 cup of milk
- ½ cup breadcrumbs
- 2 tbsp butter
- 2 large tbsp grated cheese (cheddar)
- Pepper and salt

Season the corn with pepper and salt. Stir in crumbs and beaten yolk of egg. Put mixture in buttered dish, fold in stiffly beaten egg white, then stir in cheese and milk. Put dabs of butter on top. Bake for 30 minutes in a moderate (180°C) oven.

Time taken: 40 minutes.

Conclusions
- Replace processed meats with cold, home-cooked meats on pizzas and in sandwiches to avoid additives.
- Replace flavoured instant noodles with cakes of unflavoured instant noodles and your own flavouring sauce to avoid additives.
- Opt for canned or fresh soups at the supermarket over powdered soups, which are essentially mugs of chemicals.
- Make your own stock — it's easy to save money and get rid of additives.
- Making your own risotto takes just as long as making one from the packet.
- Use some Nana recipes such as Welsh Rarebit for fast and easy meal solutions.

CHAPTER EIGHT

cakes & biscuits

make a break for it

When I was growing up, my family always had a break for morning tea or coffee. It sounds like such an old-fashioned thing to do, but in the weekends at about 11am my mother would call out, "Coffee in the lounge!" and my father, brother and I would join her and there would be instant coffee in hand-made pottery mugs, complete with not quite matching but equally as hand-made milk jug and sugar bowl and a pottery platter with some crackers and cheese, or biscuits or cake to go with the coffee.

Sometimes we'd have visitors over for "Coffee in the lounge!" but mostly it was just the four of us, sipping caffeine and munching on biscuits.

At the time it seemed like a perfectly normal thing to do and I have fond memories of sitting and talking as a family, feeling very grown up because I was allowed to drink coffee and eating nice things with it. My family is incredibly good at doing this.

My parents love nothing better than a room full of people drinking either wine or coffee and having a good old natter. Sometimes it can get a little heated, but there's always been a keen appreciation for people's views and an encouragement for people to express them.

It was probably those weekend "Coffee in the lounge!" sessions that helped me become a person who has an opinion on everything and isn't afraid to express it.

And it would be fair to say that, as my brother and I grew up, the main topic of conversation in my family was food. My brother trained as a chef, I eventually learned how to cook, both my parents have always been good cooks and we have always enjoyed sitting down and sharing our latest food findings.

To me those coffee sessions now seem like a completely out-dated ritual which has more in common with Downton Abbey than an ordinary middle-class Kiwi family in the 1970s and 1980s. There is a theory that morning and afternoon tea were invented by the upper classes in England to give themselves something to do every few hours as they idled their days away. In England "Coffee in the lounge!" would be called "Elevenses!"

In New Zealand, morning and afternoon tea breaks became a hard-won battle for labourers and farm workers who needed the sustenance provided by a "smoko".

Today, in their late seventies Mum and Dad still have "Coffee in the lounge!" and it's something I enjoy sharing with them from time to time.

In my house there is no such thing. At 11am Paul and I are usually in our separate offices in our old villa, tapping out various stories to meet a range of deadlines, having got Pearl off to school, walked the dog together, cleaned up the kitchen, hung the washing out, answered our emails and finally been able to start work.

We also rarely eat anything between meals, so the cakes, biscuits and crackers which are integral to a break for morning tea or coffee are non-existent.

Recently, I was glancing through my mother's old cooking book, where she has kept all her favourite recipes. Leaping out at me were Broken Biscuit Recipes (Uncooked), which were a regular feature of "Coffee in the lounge!", as they were easy to make along with Hokey Pokey Biscuits, Chocolate Crunch (which I made a lot), Lemon Fudge Fingers and Fudge Cake. Some of them were written into the book by me with my childlike script, using a fountain pen and I also found a quite elaborate recipe for a coconut cake in the shape of a rabbit. I remember making this for a cake competition in Form One at Northcote Intermediate School and was so pleased with it that I was sure I'd win. But I came second to a very boring lemon cake, and my mother later told me that it was because she was a teacher at the school and her daughter couldn't be seen to win the prize. I'm not sure that was true but it made me feel a little better, sort of.

If no one had been baking, then it was crackers and cheese, a favourite standby for morning tea in most homes.

Once, as a young journalist, I went to interview a family in the poorest of homes in South Auckland.

The family served me morning tea with crackers and cheese and I remember thinking how kind and generous it was of them to go to so much trouble for a lowly *Auckland Star* reporter.

Before the 1960s recipes for cakes, sponges, biscuits, loaves and scones abounded in New Zealand kitchens. According to the Ministry of Culture and Heritage, almost a third of Aunt Daisy's 1954 cookbook was devoted to "tin-fillers". It was divided into sections for particular types of baking: biscuits, large cakes (including eight types of sponge), small cakes, and "bread, scones, teacakes, etc".

But then came the advent of the supermarket, with the first Foodtown opening in Otahuhu, Auckland in June, 1958. For the first time people could buy a big range of commercially prepared baked goods at the supermarket rather than the limited offerings available at the local bakery. It led to a decline in home baking and was eagerly accepted by women who, like my mother, were beginning to join the workforce.

On the day I started school in July, 1967, my mother took herself off to teacher's training college to become a teacher. In my neighbourhood it was very unusual for the mother to go to work, and I know it was tough for Mum to stand up to those who believed a woman's place was in the home.

Consequently my mother was a very early adopter of supermarkets and the convenience they supplied for her busy life. I would head off to school with a lunchbox full of food which came in packets, while my best friend came to school with a lunchbox full of home-baked goods.

She thought my lunch was incredibly cool, and I thought her lunch looked incredibly delicious, so most days we swapped.

One of the mainstays of the supermarket baked goods has always been the Raspberry Jam Slice. I can remember it gracing our coffee mornings as a kid, and I know that occasionally I have picked it up myself to take to a children's birthday party or perhaps to serve friends for morning tea. We don't always have time to bake and these products are just one step better than pulling out a pack of biscuits. But then I picked it up one day to review it for my column.

We won't be eating Raspberry Jam Slice from the supermarket again.

I first noticed the long lists of ingredients with scary words like "solvent" and "egg replacer" in them on the back of the pack.

Raspberry Jam Slice is an old-fashioned offering, yet this modern version had a massive 45 ingredients in it. In my ancient Aunty Daisy cookbook I found a recipe for Raspberry Jam Shortcake, which is the same thing, that used just eight ingredients. So that's 37 ingredients added to this cake, mainly to give it colour and preserve it. The best-before date was a month after the date I bought it, which was also a bit of a worry.

What I also found was something I had never seen before, and haven't since, in a food product. A solvent called propylene glycol, which in large doses in animals can cause central nervous system depression and slight kidney changes. It's classified as a solvent, is also used in anti-freeze and is an anti-foaming agent. I struggled to imagine my Nana measuring bits of this into her Raspberry Jam Slice.

Then there were the four artificial colours — tartrazine, carmoisine, amaranth and ponceau 4R — which have all been banned in other countries.

Yet this is a very popular item in the baking aisle at my local supermarket. When I visited the store while I was writing this chapter I noticed about 20 packets of Raspberry Jam Slice occupied two shelves of the baking aisle alone.

IF YOU'RE NOT buying from the baking aisle, like most parents, you might be spending time in the muesli bar aisle, wondering which of the 122 varieties on offer are the best choice for your kids.

On the surface, muesli bars — full of oats and nuts — seem like a great, nutritious snack to pop in school lunches. But, hidden in those little bars can be lots of sugar and fat, emulsifiers, preservatives, flavours and colours, so you have to be careful.

And it appears some people just think "muesli" and attach the thought "healthy" and then eat heaps, believing that they are the ultimate health food.

But they really are just another form of cake or biscuit.

In 2006 *Choice* magazine in Australia found that children would be better off sitting down to a big fry-up for breakfast rather than some of the commercially produced muesli bars, which were loaded with fats and sugars.

The magazine analysed more than 150 different cereal bars and found that seven had more kilojoules than a Mars Bar and that two varieties had more saturated fat than a breakfast of two bacon rashers, two fried eggs and fried tomatoes.

Of all the bars tested, only 13 met all the analysts' healthy nutritional requirements, based on kilojoules, sugar, saturated fat, dietary fibre and wholegrain content.

A good guide when choosing a muesli bar is to look for one which has less than 2g saturated fat, less than 10g sugar, more than 1.5g fibre and less than 600kJ per bar.

I went on a mission to find such a bar and was happy to find a Nice and Natural Nut Bar which not only met these criteria but also only took 10, all natural ingredients, to make them.

See my analysis below for some healthy and not so healthy cakes, bars and biscuits.

Nutritionists will advise you to keep cakes, biscuits and bars to a minimum and regard them as a treat food, something you don't have every day and certainly not as a snack.

Instead they advise you to make healthy snacks for yourself and your children, such as yoghurt topped with fresh fruit, fruit or celery with peanut butter, humus and corn chips, nuts and dried fruit.

My Findings: Cakes and Biscuits

Oki Doki Disco Bars

- Despite its disco fever packaging, no artificial colours to worry about.
- Uses cocoa butter, which indicates good quality chocolate.
- Very high in sugar.

One Square Meal

- A feat of food science, providing exactly 33 per cent of all your nutritional and energy needs for one day.
- Some clarity needed with the labelling.
- Great for busy people, but not something you'd want to eat three times a day.

Raspberry Jam Slice

- Contains four artificial colours which have been banned in other countries.
- Takes 45 ingredients to make something which, if baked at home, would take eight.
- Has a very long "best before" date which is scary for a baked product.

Collisions Mint Treats

- No artificial flavours, colours or preservatives.
- Nearly half the biscuit is made up of sugar.
- Uses natural flavour.

Le Snak Cheese

- It takes seven ingredients to process the cheese to ensure it lasts four months on the shelf without refrigeration.
- You can save on additives and cash by substituting real cheese with bought crackers.
- Each serve contains about 1 teaspoon of fat.

Milkies Choc Vanilla

- Has an astounding 31 ingredients for a bar the size of a finger.
- Has two "faux fibre" ingredients (inulin and polydextrose) which are not the same as the fibre you find in fruit, veges and grains.
- You pay a high processed food price for the low fat and sugar content.

Krispies

- It takes eight ingredients to make these biscuits, which is similar to the number required if you made them yourself.
- One serving will provide you with about 85 calories.
- A true Kiwi biscuit, produced here since the 1950s.

Ryvita Fruit and Seed Crunch with Honey

- These are so good for you they should be available free on prescription from your doctor.
- Completely free of artificial additives with only eight ingredients.
- Very high in fibre from wholegrains, seeds and fruit.

Nice & Natural Nut Bar Original

- One of the few products not to hide ingredients behind the food label codes. What you read is what you get.
- Contains high oleic peanuts which have more heart healthy oleic fatty acid in them at higher levels than olive oil.
- Only 10 ingredients and all natural as far as I can tell.

Arnott's Iced Animals

- Half a teaspoon of sugar in each tiny biscuit.
- Three artificial colours which are banned in other countries.
- Artificial flavours.

Arnott's Tiny Teddy Chocolate Biscuits

- Reformulated to have fewer kilojoules and less saturated fat and more fibre.
- No artificial preservatives, but still has artificial flavours and colour.
- Australian school canteen guidelines say they are okay once a day.

— *my recipes* —

Mum's Broken Biscuits (Uncooked) Orange Fudge

    1 x 250g packet wine biscuits
    ¾ cup coconut
    grated rind of an orange
    125g butter
    ½ tin sweetened condensed milk

Crush biscuits and mix with coconut and orange rind. Melt butter and condensed milk together and add to dry ingredients. Press into greased tin and refrigerate. Use juice of ½ orange to make icing.

    Time taken: 10 minutes plus refrigeration.

Fudge Cake

1 x 250g packet arrowroot biscuits
1 tbsp cocoa
1 cup coconut
1 cup mixed fruit and nuts (chopped)
½ tin sweetened condensed milk
125g butter

Crush biscuits and mix with coconut, cocoa and mixed fruit and nuts. Melt butter and sweetened condensed milk, then pour onto the dried ingredients and mix well. Press into greased tin and refrigerate.

Time taken: 10 minutes plus refrigeration.

Lemon Fudge Fingers

1 x 250g packet wine biscuits
1 cup coconut
½ tin sweetened condensed milk
125g butter

Crush biscuits and mix with the coconut. Melt butter and sweetened condensed milk together and pour on dry ingredients. Press into greased tin and refrigerate. Ice with lemon icing.

Time Taken: 10 minutes plus refrigeration.

Oat Fudge Squares

1 cup rolled oats
1 ½ cups boiling water
75g butter
1 tsp vanilla

1 cup flour
¼ cup cocoa
1 ¼ cup sugar
1 tsp baking soda
2 eggs

Put oats in a bowl with boiling water. Chop up butter and add to oats with vanilla. Set aside, while you sift flour, cocoa, sugar and baking soda into a big bowl. Add oat mixture and eggs and beat until smooth.

Pour into a greased tin and bake for 35 minutes at 180°C. Cool for 10 minutes in the tin then tip out to cool completely. When it's cold, ice with chocolate icing. Cut into squares.

Time taken: 1 hour.

Hokey Pokey Biscuits

125g butter
125g sugar
1 tbsp golden syrup
1 tsp baking powder
1 cup flour

Cream together butter and sugar.

Put golden syrup in a pot and bring to the boil. Add baking powder and mix into the creamed butter and sugar. Add flour, mix all together then put on a cold greased oven tray in teaspoon lots allowing room to spread. Cook in a 180°C oven until golden.

Time taken: 30 minutes.

Cheese Frizzles

These are a fabulous old biscuit which I discovered when a *Woman's Weekly* reader sent me her Grandma's old domestic science notebook from 1944. They were a huge hit in my house and will be in yours as well I'm sure. If you can't find fine oatmeal just whizz up normal rolled oats in the food processor until they are fine.

> 4 tbsp fine oatmeal
> 4 tbsp grated cheese (I used tasty)
> 2 tbsp flour
> ¼ tsp mustard powder
> ¼ tsp salt
> Ground pepper
> 4 tbsp fat for frying (I used lard but olive oil or butter will do)
> 2 tsp baking powder.

Mix all the ingredients together except the baking powder. Add enough cold water to mix to a stiff batter. If it looks like porridge, it is too liquid and the frizzles will flatten out in the frying pan. If this happens, as it did to mine, just add a bit more oatmeal.

Melt the fat in the frying pan until it spits if you put a drop of water in it, and add the baking powder to the mix just before you are about to start cooking.

Drop teaspoonfuls into the hot fat. They will bubble a bit like crumpets. Turn over and cook until golden on both sides.

Drain on paper towels and serve on their own or spread with fish or meat paste.

Time taken: 30 minutes.

Cheese Biscuits

This is one of my favourite recipes from my Mum's cookbook.

    1 cup plain flour
    1/8 tsp cayenne pepper
    ½ cup butter
    1 cup grated cheese
    1 tsp claret or burgundy
    ¼ tsp Worcestershire sauce
    Chutney

Sift flour and cayenne into a bowl and rub in the butter and cheese. Mix to a dry dough with wine and Worcestershire sauce.

    Form a long roll, wrap in greaseproof paper and chill in fridge until firm.

    Cut in slices and place on a greased tray.

    Drop a little chutney in the centre of each and bake in a 180°C oven for 10 to 12 minutes.

    Time taken: 30 minutes plus refrigeration.

Cheese Crackers

This is a very old recipe with just a few ingredients which tastes amazing.

    2 cups flour
    90g butter
    ¾ cup grated tasty cheese
    water
    ½ tsp salt

Sift the flour into a bowl and then rub in the butter until it resembles breadcrumbs. Add the cheese and salt and mix with enough water to form a dough. Knead for a few moments until it is soft and smooth. Roll out until very thin. You may have to do this in batches.

Cut into shapes — I like squares because there is no waste, as there is with circles. Place on a greased baking tray then prick each with a fork and bake for five minutes in a 180°C oven or until golden and crisp.

When completely cool, store in an airtight container.

Muesli Bars

1 ½ cups quick cooking oats
½ cup unsweetened shredded coconut
½ cup chopped craisins (cranberry raisins) and a handful of raisins (any dried fruit will work)
½ cup maple syrup or honey
½ cup peanut butter (or any nut butter)
2 tbsp ground flax seed
1 tsp cinnamon
2 tsp vanilla extract

Combine all the ingredients in a bowl. The mix should blend together well but if too dry add a bit of olive oil. Press into a tin and freeze. After a few hours, cut up while semi-frozen. Wrap the bars in plastic wrap and keep in the freezer.

Sandwiches

In the days when people gathered together for morning and afternoon teas the sandwich was a delicate affair, not the huge doorstop mounds of bread and variety of fillings we buy today. In Nana's time, sandwiches were finger food, cut into delicate shapes and filled with delectable pastes, potted meats and salads to tempt the taste buds. These days you might find Nana sandwiches at a high tea put on by a hotel chain, at funerals or at bridge parties but perhaps it's time we brought back the tradition of serving them in our homes with tea. Here are some recipes to try, and you never know, your kids might like them in their lunchboxes as well.
I've omitted the very popular recipe for Brain Paste which I found repeated many times in my old recipe books.

Potted Tomato Paste

    3 ripe tomatoes
    Pepper and salt
    50g butter
    1 small onion finely chopped
    50g grated cheese
    100g breadcrumbs
    1 egg beaten

Peel the tomatoes and chop. Put in a saucepan with salt and pepper, butter and onion and cook until tender. Mash until smooth and then add the egg, cheese and breadcrumbs, stirring quickly until thick.

Sardine Paste

    1 tin of sardines in oil (about 100g)
    1 tsp anchovy sauce (fish sauce is a good substitute)
    1 tsp tomato sauce
    1 hard-boiled egg
    1 tsp parsley or chives finely chopped
    malt vinegar

Tip the sardines with their oil into a pot and heat until warm, mashing with a fork, then add the anchovy or fish sauce and tomato sauce. Mash up the hard-boiled egg and mix in with the sardines. When cold, add the finely chopped herbs and a few drops of malt vinegar.

Ever Ready Paste

This old recipe uses herrings, but you can substitute any oily fish, such as mackerel, mullet or kahawai.

    1 mullet, mackerel or kahawai, skinned, boned and filleted.
    3 eggs
    100g butter
    2 tbsp cream
    A pinch cayenne pepper to taste
    ½ tsp ground pepper

Cook the fish fillets in a little water, then mince (either use a hand mincer or your food processor). Beat the eggs then add the minced fish, cream, cayenne and pepper. Put the mixture in a greased basin in a saucepan of hot water and simmer for 15 minutes. Put the mixture in clean jars and when cool cover with some melted butter.

You can also use smoked fish for this recipe, and you only need to take the flesh off the skin and mince it, there is no need to cook it first.

Cheese and Salmon Paste

    1 tin of salmon (210g)
    1 tbsp butter (room temperature)
    1 tsp mustard
    100g cheese, grated
    Salt and pepper
    1 tsp lemon juice

Drain the liquid from the tin of salmon and reserve. Mash up the fish, removing any bones or skin. Add the butter, mustard, cheese and pepper and salt to taste. Mix all together well and then stir through the lemon juice. If the mixture is a bit dry, drizzle back in a little of the salmon liquid you reserved earlier. Spoon into clean jars and store in the fridge.

Vegetarian Potted Meat

    1 tin borlotti or white beans, drained
    50g breadcrumbs
    25g cheese grated
    1 tsp finely chopped onion
    25g butter
    Large pinch of dried herbs
    Salt to taste
    Pinch of cayenne

Pinch of grated nutmeg
2 tsp soy sauce

Combine all the ingredients in a food processor or mash together. Adjust seasonings if necessary. Spoon into clean jars and store in the fridge.

Nuts and Raisins

1 cup raisins
1 cup walnuts
Lemon juice
Cream

Chop the nuts and raisins until very fine and then moisten with a little lemon juice and cream of equal quantities. Spread between buttered wholemeal bread. You could replace the cream in this recipe with sour cream for extra flavour.

*For the best presentation remove the crusts from your sandwiches and use cookie cutters to cut them into rounds or squares.

*To keep sandwiches from drying out, drape a moist piece of muslin or tea-towel over them, or cover with lettuce leaves.

CONCLUSIONS
- Supermarket baked goods can contain many added preservatives, colourings and flavours which you won't find in homemade goods.
- Muesli may be healthy, but muesli bars may not.
- Aim for less than 2g saturated fat, less than 10g sugar, more than 1.5g fibre and less than 600kJ per muesli bar.
- "Filling the tins" used to be something women did once a week to keep their family supplied with cakes and biscuits. Why not do the same and get your kids to help you in the kitchen at the weekend.
- You could probably do it once a month if you put some in the freezer.
- Sandwiches used to contain delicious pastes — see if your children like some of the old-fashioned offerings.

without tricks

When I was a busy mother working outside the home, I was conscious of the fact that when I walked through the front door at 6pm if I was clutching something brightly coloured and regarded as a treat the smiling faces of my children did wonders to alleviate any guilt I might have been feeling for not being with them.

I'm sure it's a common feeling among working mothers who are not always there to share after school meals and who may not have cooked their dinner.

When my first two children were quite young I was 30 years old and working as the editor of a top-selling women's magazine called *Woman's Day*.

I would often clip recipes from my own magazine, come home after work laden down with groceries and set about cooking something trendy and new with 10 different ingredients and the requirement that I jump through several hoops to cook it. All this after a long and stressful day at work.

Somewhere deep inside of me was a need to use

food to show them that I cared about them. Today, I see cooking and feeding a family as one of the most nurturing and, by extension, fulfilling things a woman can do.

But in those days, I was just trying to do something special.

In the end my first husband, Anthony, sat me down after one of these outrageous culinary feats which had ended up being served at 7pm, half an hour before the kids' bedtime and had a chat.

"These meals you are cooking are really nice. But you know the kids are just really happy eating basic food for dinner. Mince, sausages, potatoes, frozen veges. The stuff I cook for them," he said kindly.

"I know, but I just want to spoil them, cook something special now and again."

"Don't take this the wrong way, but I think they'd rather you walked in the front door and sat on the couch with them for a few hours. They miss you."

I promptly burst into tears, which I don't think was the reaction Anthony was intending. And I realised that he was right. I was far better off dropping my bags and making straight for the couch for cuddles, homework, bath, book and bed.

Throughout the 12 years I spent working long hours for big media companies and trying to be a good mother, I never got rid of the guilt. I think that the main reason I gave up my full-time career and moved home to work as a freelance writer nine years ago was because my two older kids were in their teens and I believe teenagers need you just as much if not more than they need you as babies. And my last child, Pearl, had just started school, and I didn't think I could face not being there after school for yet another child. I needed to be with my kids and working from home gave me the chance to do that.

And I cooked. Like a mad woman. I might as well have had a T shirt printed which said "Nurture is my middle name."

THE SIGNATURE TREAT food for children has always been something sweet and cold from the freezer. Many parents have for years bought plastic tubes of flavoured and brightly coloured liquid and stored them in the freezer to be distributed to eager children on hot summer afternoons.

I was one of those parents in the 80s who liked to give the kids something special. In my defence, my knowledge of food additives back then was very poor, and my children got through a hell of a lot of these.

When I recently bought a pack home to look at, my son, Daniel, saw them sitting on the kitchen table and picked them up with glee, before informing me that he never really liked the "fairy floss force field" flavour but "bubblegum quasar" was his favourite.

I prevented him from putting them in the freezer and took them off to my office to analyse. When I'd finished, I picked them up, walked outside and threw them in the rubbish bin, far away from hungry 26-year-olds looking for reminders of their childhood.

Before I threw them out, I spent five minutes shaking my head in disbelief. If you had asked me to compile a list of the worst artificial colours to feed your children, the colours used in these ice treats would be them.

Five out of the six artificial colours have been banned in other countries, including the US and the UK. One colour, amaranth, has been banned in the US since 1976. One preservative has been phased out of Diet Coke due to health concerns. And all eight flavours are achieved by using artificial flavours.

I felt really angry that this product was allowed to sit on our supermarket shelves, where unsuspecting parents would pick it up and deliver it to their children thinking they were giving them a harmless treat.

Of all the products I have analysed so far for "Wendyl Wants to Know", this one was the most disgusting and I was left wondering how products like these actually make it on to our shelves. Surely, even the most ill-informed bureaucrat in our Ministry of Health would be able to see that these are sailing close to the wind when it comes to nutrition (none), natural ingredients (none) and safe (hardly) foods being put out there for the public to consume.

I came to the conclusion that, if you give one of these tubes to your child, you are essentially feeding them water, sugar, and a chemical cocktail of flavours and colours which cannot be recommended by anyone interested in a healthy diet.

FORTUNATELY THERE ARE some companies working very hard to bring healthy treats to your family. In the freezer section of your supermarket, you should be able to find alternative ice treats which clearly state "no artificial flavours, colourings or preservatives". And if you're lucky, your supermarket might stock Smooze, which are a delight to have in the house. They taste good, are dairy-free and have no artificial colours, flavourings or preservatives. Many kids who are dairy-free and can only eat ice-blocks crave the taste of ice-cream, and these do a really good job of tasting just like ice-cream but with coconut milk instead of cow's milk. Their size means children are unlikely to overeat, for what is essentially a snack treat, and call me adventurous, but I like the flavours, which encourage children to get away from the traditional, and often artificially flavoured, treat flavours of raspberry or orange. These come with pink guava, pineapple and passionfruit and encourage children to extend their tastebuds a little.

You can also make your own ice treats really easily using flavoured milks. You can get chocolate, strawberry and banana milks in the supermarket which don't have any artificial colours or flavours, so go for those. Simply pour them into an ice block mould, freeze and your kids will love them.

Or you can use fruit juice or a drink mix (again go for no artificial flavours or colours).

The best thing about making these yourself is that the colours tend to be pastel pinks or yellows rather than bright almost fluorescent colours not often found in nature, such as blue, purple and green. I think it's good for kids to get used to connecting the colour of their food to natural ingredients.

Another treat food for kids is lollies and sweets. In our house we had two incorrigibly sweet-toothed kids, Daniel and Alex. They could get through an amazing amount of lollies in one sitting and devoted most of their pocket money to them as kids.

We never tried to ban them, but we did attempt to keep them as treat foods, which means something you don't have every day.

Alex discovered that you could cook your own sweets when she grew older and would make gorgeous fudge and coconut ice for us all, making sure she had a good stash for herself.

When you're a grandmother you technically have to have a lolly jar. It lives in your pantry and your grand-daughter sticks her little hands inside and retrieves one lolly for each little fist, which she clutches to herself with absolute joy before inspecting and then popping them into her mouth one by one. The problem for modern day grandmothers is that choosing the right lolly brings up all sorts of dilemmas. We all know lollies are a treat food, but even treat food needs to be the best it can be for the little darlings. So no artificial flavours, colours or preservatives are a must. But when it comes to sugar, the main attraction of lollies is that they are sweet, so there's no cutting corners on that.

The only lollies which make it into my house are made by the Natural Confectionery Company. I analysed their jelly babies and was very impressed that this company hasn't done what so many others do and labelled their product as "natural" while slipping in colourings and flavourings which might be naturally derived but still have huge question marks over them, if you do your research. All their colourings and flavourings get a clear tick as being truly natural and unlikely to cause any health reactions in your children.

These days we rarely make our own lollies or sweets, as it is so much easier to buy them ready-made. But in Nana's day it wasn't unusual to churn out a few blackballs or barley sugars from the kitchen.

A few years ago I was asked by a *Woman's Weekly* reader to find her a recipe for old-fashioned mints. "They have no 'crisp coating' on the outside and they melt in your mouth with a delicious mint flavour," she said.

It took me a while, but I eventually found a recipe and made them up one afternoon. They turned out to be delicious little soft morsels, which were very delicate, and I could just see them presented in a little crystal dish after dinner at my Nana's house or even at Downton Abbey.

I make these often, and I hope you enjoy them as much as we do.

Barley sugars are an old-fashioned boiled sweet which uses barley more for the flavour than for any health reasons. I made these up after a very ragged piece of paper fell out of an old recipe book I was thumbing through. It was in very old-fashioned hand writing and I felt that it had been well used to make barley sugars time and time again and so I had to try it out (recipe below).

My Findings: Treats

Zooper Dooper Flavoured Ice Confection Mix — 8 Cosmic Flavours

I made a rule not to give a full analysis of foods in this book as it would end up reading more like a text book than something which I hope is enjoyable as well as informative. But in this case I think you need to read the full list and treat the experience as a shocking indictment on the lack of responsibility shown by the people we trust to bring us healthy food. The Ministry of Health and the owners of your supermarkets who willingly place these on their shelves and make a profit out of selling them to parents to feed to their children.

Ingredients (in order of greatest quantity):
- *Water*
- *Sugar*
- *Food Acid (330)*

    This is citric acid which is a common food additive and considered quite safe.
- *Preservatives (211, 202, 223)*

    The first preservative is sodium benzoate (211) and there's not much wrong with it on its own, but there have been concerns that when mixed with certain artificial colours- three of which are listed below (sunset yellow 110, tartrazine 102 and carmoisine 122) it may be linked to hyperactive behaviour. A study by Southampton University tested sodium benzoate with artificial colours and found some evidence of hyperactivity but that the results were inconsistent, and so there are further studies going on. However, in 2008 Coca-Cola phased it out of Diet Coke, due to concerns that sodium benzoate was linked to damage to DNA and hyperactivity.

Potassium sorbate (202) is the potassium salt of sorbic acid which is considered quite safe, but some people have an intolerance to sodium metabisulphite (223) and asthmatics are advised to avoid it.

- *Flavours*

There are eight different flavours in this packet, which go by the following names — cola cosmos, deep space lime, fairy floss force field, blackcurrant phaser, raspberry rocket, bubblegum quasar, space pineapple and orange quadrant. Unlike artificial colourings, artificial flavours do not need to be named or listed, which is extremely frustrating as it makes it very difficult to ascertain if any have health issues attached to them. Which means you are feeding your child an unknown mix of chemicals designed to taste and smell like space pineapples, etc.

- *Colours (102, 110, 122, 123, 133, 150d)*

Five out of the six artificial colours listed here have been banned in other countries. One has been banned in the United States since 1976. And the sixth colour has major health question marks over it. Yet Food Standards Australia and New Zealand (FSANZ) allows all of them to be used in our foods.

- Tartrazine (102) is an artificial yellow dye which has been banned in Norway and the United Kingdom due to links to hyperactivity in children, revealed in the same study mentioned under sodium benzoate. FSANZ says that in Australia (where this product is made) food manufacturers use lower levels than those used in the UK study. "For example, the UK study assumed a concentration of 67 mg/kg of the colour tartrazine in confectionery, whereas the average concentration of tartrazine found in confectionery in the FSANZ survey was only 10 mg/kg," it says. Therefore it allows the colouring in our foods.
- Sunset Yellow FCF (110) is banned in Norway and Finland. After the same study mentioned for tartrazine, the United Kingdom requested a voluntary withdrawal of this colouring in all its foods, and it is thought that most foods manufactured in the UK do not use this colouring anymore.
- Carmoisine (122) is a red synthetic coal tar dye, which has been banned in Canada, Japan, Norway, Sweden and the United States. It can cause allergic reactions.
- Amaranth (123) is a dark red or purple dye which is a suspected carcinogen banned in the USA in 1976 as well as in Russia, Norway and Austria. It is also restricted in France and Italy. The ban on amaranth in the United States and several other countries was the result of numerous studies citing links to cancer in

laboratory animals as well as birth defects, stillbirths, sterility and early foetal death. It is not recommended for consumption by children and is considered very dangerous as it increases hyperactivity in affected children.

- Brilliant Blue (133) is another synthetic coal tar dye, which was banned in Belgium, France, Germany, Switzerland, Sweden, Austria and Norway because of concerns it is a carcinogen, but that ban has since been lifted. However it is banned in Argentina, Bulgaria, Czech Republic, France, Hungary, Italy, Mauritius, Morocco, Poland, Portugal, Trinidad and Turkey.

- Caramel IV (150d) is a highly controversial colour which has nothing to do with caramel but is made out of reacting corn sugar with ammonia and sulphites under high pressures and high temperatures. Those reactions produce the chemicals 2- methylimidazole and 4-methylimidazole (4-MEI). The Centre for Science in the Public Interest (CSPI), a Washington-based consumer watchdog group, has petitioned the US Food and Drug Administration to ban this colouring on the grounds that the chemicals are carcinogenic. A 2007 study by the National Toxicology Program found "clear evidence" of lung tumours in mice. However the American Beverage Association insists that it is not a threat to human health, there is no evidence that it causes cancer in humans and a lawsuit has been filed to block efforts to list 4-MEI as a carcinogen.

Smooze

- A great ice-cream tasting treat for dairy-free kids.
- Unlike other throw-in-the-freezer treats, these have no artificial flavours, colours or preservatives.
- Each serving is a sensible size of just 65ml — enough for a light snack without over-feeding your child on unnecessary calories.

The Natural Confectionery Co. Jelly Babies

These are mainly sugar and jelly with natural flavours and colours added. Five of these jelly babies will deliver three teaspoons of sugar but in my opinion depriving a child entirely of lollies will just set up a demand for them, which they will find whether you like it or not next time they are at their friend's house, or their grandmother's. So I believe that occasionally a lolly or two as a special treat is a good idea, and these make a good choice for that lolly jar.

SUMMARY:
- Genuine natural flavourings and colours, and no preservatives.
- Five of these jelly babies will deliver three teaspoons of sugar.
- A great choice for occasional treats.

—my recipes—

Ice Treats

Buy yourself a good ice treat maker. I found one produced by Zoku which makes three ice blocks at a time in five minutes. You keep it in the freezer and when you're ready click the sticks in place, pour the mixture in and leave to set for five minutes. The grandchildren love the suspense and get very excited: when you pull out a freshly made ice block they love it. I first saw one of these in New York but it was very heavy so I didn't want to lug it back home. I was delighted to find it on Trade Me and have been glad I bought it ever since.

Ice Block Mixes

- Flavoured milks
- Blend some fresh fruit, such as banana, strawberry, mango, peach or plum with some yoghurt and milk to make a smoothie, and then pour into moulds.
- Mix up some packet drinks (do check they have no artificial flavours or colours).
- Use fresh fruit juices.

Alex's Fudge

    3 cups sugar
    ½ cup milk

½ x 400g can sweetened condensed milk
125g butter
2 tbsp golden syrup
1 tsp vanilla essence
Pinch salt

Grease a 20cm square cake tin with butter. Place all the fudge ingredients in a saucepan and bring to the boil, stirring regularly until melted together.

Simmer mixture hard for 20 minutes. Keep whisking to stop the mixture sticking and burning.

Remove from the heat, pour into prepared tin and leave to set. Cut into small squares to serve.

Alex's Coconut Ice

100g butter
1 cup milk
6 cups icing sugar
1 tsp salt
1 cup desiccated coconut
2 tsp coconut essence

Place the butter, milk, icing sugar and salt in a large saucepan and heat gently until the sugar dissolves. Bring the mixture to the boil and keep the heat sufficient to just maintain the boil, stirring only occasionally, until the mixture reaches soft-ball stage (120°C).

Add the coconut and coconut essence and remove from the heat. Cool for 5–10 minutes, then beat until the mixture thickens. Pour into a greased tin, approximately 20x20cm. Allow to cool and cut into squares.

Traditionally you would colour half the mixture pink with food colouring but unless you can find a natural food colouring just leave them white.

Old-Fashioned Granny Peppermints

You will need to source some good quality peppermint essential oil to get the strength of flavour needed for these. You can purchase it at health shops and chemists. Do make sure the label says "essential oil", which means it has come from a peppermint plant, not "fragrance" which means it is an artificial oil and not something you should consume.

- 1 egg white
- 250g icing sugar
- 150g caster sugar
- 1 tsp peppermint essential oil

Beat the egg white until stiff, then fold into the icing sugar. Add the caster sugar and the peppermint. You should get a stiff paste — add more sugar until you do. Roll into little balls and leave overnight to set.

Peppermint fans should check when buying peppermint flavoured lollies or chocolate that "peppermint oil" is listed in the ingredients panel as a flavouring. This means you are getting real peppermint in the flavouring not artificial.

Barley Sugars

　　　100g pearl barley
　　　Rind of ½ lemon
　　　1.5 litres of cold water
　　　700g sugar
　　　Juice of 1 lemon

Put the barley, lemon rind and water in a pot. Bring to the boil and then leave to simmer for two hours. Set aside to cool.

　　　Tip the mixture into a sieve lined with some muslin or fine cloth. Measure out 600ml of the strained liquid and put it into another saucepan.

　　　Add the sugar to the barley liquid and put on a low heat, stirring until the sugar has dissolved. Bring to the boil but do not stir. When it starts to boil, add the lemon juice and boil the syrup until it reaches what is called the "soft crack" stage. This means that when you drop some of the syrup into cold water it will solidify into threads which you can still bend when you remove them before breaking. If they crack you have gone too far and have made brittle toffee, which is still really nice. (Just pour into a pan and then crack with a hammer when it is set.)

　　　Pour the syrup into a well-greased sponge tin and, when cool enough to handle, oil some kitchen scissors and use these to cut the mixture into strips about 5cm long. Hold each strip by the ends and twist to form spirals. Work quickly, as you will only be able to do this before the barley sugar sets. Place on a piece of baking paper to set completely. Enjoy!

CONCLUSIONS
- It's easy to believe that showering our kids with food treats might make up for the guilt you feel for having a job and not being around all the time. But just spending some time with them on the couch is all they really want.
- Just because a product is on the supermarket shelves does not mean it is good for you. Be vigilant and don't trust Big Food to look after you.
- Treats are good occasionally, but do make sure they are the best ones you can buy or make.
- Food doesn't come in fluoro colours in nature, so it shouldn't in your house. Teach your kids that.

CHAPTER TEN

drinks

hard to swallow

Occasionally, the new editor at the *Weekend Herald*, Andrew Laxon, sends me suggestions for my column. I'm always happy to get ideas from him. It's the least I can do in return for his patience when I'm occasionally a little late handing in my column.

He sent an email once which simply said: "What about doing Coke v Pepsi head to head some time?"

"What a great idea," I thought to myself. "Popular drinks, millions of litres consumed around the world every day, what's the difference?"

By the time I'd finished analysing them, I suggested that next time he made a suggestion he might want to opt for something a little less taxing on my time. Not only had I spent far too long bogged down on the issue of the colouring both beverages use (see end of the chapter for my findings) but at my suggestion we ran the column past a lawyer, which took a lot of time also. I must have put him off, because he hasn't made a suggestion since.

THE BIG PROBLEM with the drinks we and our children consume is sugar. Whether it's Coke, Pepsi, L&P, or any number of energy or sports drinks, the sugar levels in them are high (see my chart of the sugar levels of drinks I have analysed at the end of the chapter for a quick guide).

Too much sugar in our diet leads to problems such as obesity and diabetes, which are two of the biggest health issues facing New Zealanders today. High sugar levels also boost cholesterol and increase the risk of various heart problems in children. Then there is tooth decay.

After my column on Coke and Pepsi was published, I received an email from a dentist concerned that I hadn't mentioned the impact carbonated beverages have on the teeth of young people.

"The major problem that was not given any consideration was the acidity (measured by pH) of these drinks. They have a very deleterious effect on the enamel of teeth by a process of demineralisation. This is especially so if there is a constant intake over a medium to long term," he said.

Another recent study, from the US Centers for Disease Control and Prevention, found that boys consumed an average of 361 calories of added sugar each day. For girls, the daily average was 282. I found it most interesting that most of the added sugars were consumed at home.

So with obesity, diabetes, heart disease and tooth decay staring us in the face why do we continue to drink — and let our kids consume — these drinks?

On the extremely rare occasions that I buy one it is because I am thirsty, out and about and need something refreshing. Which means the many bottles of water available in the dairy fridge should suffice. But then something else kicks in. The fact that I'm in a dairy, and since I was a child, dairies always meant treats. And so I head for the fridge and choose something sweet, which is usually a sparkling juice if I can find it.

The desire to eat sugar is a mixture of satisfying taste, giving ourselves pleasure and getting satisfaction for most people. And perhaps this flows over to how we act as parents when we let our children choose one of these drinks.

Trends in beverage consumption among children and adolescents over the past few decades suggest the consumption of soft drinks is increasing and that they may be replacing more nutritious beverages, such as milk and fruit juices.

In the United States, 12- to 19-year-old females have doubled, and males have tripled, their consumption of soft drinks and have reduced their consumption of milk by more than 40 per cent in the past two decades, according to a report by the Australian National Health and Medical Research Council. And an Otago University survey found that 37 per cent of New Zealand adults were overweight and 28 per cent obese.

The percentage of overweight people has been increasing slowly but steadily, from 34 per cent in 1977. The obese category has expanded much faster, nearly tripling from 10 per cent in the same period.

Some of that will be the result of eating junk food and processed food, but a lot of it will be soft drinks and that means sugar.

So what can we do about it? Many people turn to diet drinks, which use artificial sweeteners to replace sugar. I've written a whole chapter about artificial sweeteners, so you can go there to see the reasons why I won't go near them. It's a bit like my view on butter vs margarine. Sugar is natural, artificial sweeteners are not.

Recently Pearl had her 14th birthday party. She had invited 18 girls around for the afternoon and they all had to dress up.

"What food do you want to have?" I asked a few days before.

"Just some pizza, and then can I go to the supermarket and get some drinks and things?"

I watched with interest as she unpacked her treats.

There were the usual lollies, but she had selected ones with no artificial colours, flavours or preservatives. Good girl. There was chocolate, which was pretty good as well. And then there was a 12-pack of Coke, and a 12-pack of a variety of soft drinks with LITE written clearly on the label.

"Why these?" I asked her and her friend who was helping her unpack everything.

"I just thought it might be better not to have too much sugar," she said.

"Good thinking," I said, picking up the box to see which artificial sweeteners had been used instead.

As I did this the girls helped themselves to a can each to try.

Neither of them could finish the cans. In fact they each only took one sip before pronouncing their choice "disgusting".

"It tastes all right going down but then there's a bitter aftertaste."

Sound familiar? If you are not a drinker of diet drinks, which I am not, when you try one it really tastes quite horrific. There's a nasty bitter, dry, almost tingly aftertaste in your mouth which is hard to think of as a normal experience.

"Why would you drink something which tastes so horrible?" I ask Paul on the rare occasion he orders one when we are out.

"No calories," is his reply.

"No nutrition, no taste, no enjoyment, no good." I reply. It's become a bit of a mantra.

And then I found a study from the University of Texas Health Science Center, San Antonio, which looked at 1550 people over eight years and found that people only drinking diet soft drinks had a higher risk of obesity. This might be due to the fact that they were going to McDonald's and ordering a Big Mac, big fries and a diet Coke.

A study from the University of North Carolina at Chapel Hill found that when people swapped their favourite sugary soft drink for the diet variety, they ate more desserts and more bread than people who swapped their go-to beverage for water. It appears that artificial sweeteners may increase your hunger for sweet things.

Or it might be that artificial sweeteners create some other reaction in the body.

As I am writing this a new study has found a link between diet soft drinks and heart disease.

The *Journal of General Internal Medicine* released a study which looked at 2564 adults over 40 living in Manhattan. Researchers found that diet and regular soft drink consumption were both associated with a number of risk factors for cardiovascular disease.

The researchers found that daily consumption of diet soda was still independently associated with an increased risk for stroke, heart attack and death. The reasons for the association are unclear, the authors said, and the results must be interpreted with caution.

One of the authors told people not to be alarmed as there was still a chance there were other unmeasured variables. But I did like her statement that: "If people stop drinking diet soda, they are not going to be missing out on any important vitamins or minerals."

Exactly.

So, if we're not going down the diet soda track, what's another alternative to getting rid of sugar-laden drinks from our diets?

I think that, like much else I do in my life, it comes down to looking at what Nana did before the American servicemen introduced her and her friends to Coke during World War II.

In my home I make sure that there is a massive filtered water container in my fridge at all times. I'm not going to go into the argument about tap water versus filtered water because for the purposes of this chapter it's all about taste. Filtered water just tastes better than tap water, which has a very distinct chlorine taste where I live. Cold water is also very enjoyable.

I also have a Sodastream machine and make sparkling water which I keep in the fridge.

I know this works well because I'm refilling both water supplies most days as my family drinks up both kinds.

I also make sun tea out of herbal teabags, which goes down well with adults and children when poured fresh from a jug in the fridge (Do check which herbs you are giving to your children first. Most fruit teas are fine.)

One of the things I love most about travelling in the United States is that you can always get an iced tea without sugar, unlike the iced teas for sale here, which are laden with sugar.

So I make that for myself and keep that in the fridge.

I sometimes make a very old recipe called lemon water, which is a much tastier version of water and not unlike the flavoured waters you can buy at the dairy.

And encourage everyone in your house to dilute fruit juice half and half with water to reduce the amount of sugar they are consuming. They won't notice the difference after a while.

My Findings

Monster Energy – 500ml

As parents we all know energy drinks shouldn't be consumed by children, yet they love them and the drinks seem to be directly marketed at young teens, with their advertising using extreme sports, video games and hip hop music to send their youth consumption message. The problem is that a 12-year-old buying a drink to quench their thirst also ingests high amounts of caffeine and sugar. This brand was nominated to me by a bunch of 12-year-olds as the most popular in their group of friends. Caffeine is not something children, including teenagers, should be consuming yet many children can be seen coming out of dairies having just bought energy drinks containing the stuff.

My advice is to educate your child away from the perception that these drinks are good for you because they have added herbs and use words like "supplements", and talk to them about why caffeine does not belong in their diet. Encourage them to choose flavoured waters which are easily available.

Summary
- Caffeine is an important component of energy drinks like this. They're great for your hangover but should not be consumed by your children.
- Additives such as taurine, ginseng and guarana are unlikely to be at high enough levels to have any health benefit.

- Nearly 12 tsp of sugar in one serving is far too high and well over the 40g per day most health professionals recommend.
- At 500ml this is really two servings for a child, but is listed as one.

Coke Vs Pepsi — 1 litre

In New Zealand it is often cheaper to buy a bottle of Coca-Cola or Pepsi than it is to buy milk.

This is of concern to health professionals who advise that drinks like this should be limited when given to children.

Researching these products took me on a journey to many studies which either blamed these drinks for obesity, calcium deficiency and cancer-causing chemicals or defended them.

Personally I take a "where there's smoke there's fire" approach to controversial ingredients and avoid them, but you can make up your own mind from the information available.

What is a certainty is that children and teenagers worldwide are drinking more soft drinks and less milk and fruit juice which provide valuable nutrients.

And every health professional will advise that these two drinks should be considered as occasional treat foods rather than as a regular feature in the diet.

If your child loves fizzy drinks, then my advice is to buy a Sodastream and make your own, using fruit juice or a fruit syrup as the flavouring, to reduce sugar intake, and avoid artificial colours, flavours and preservatives and increase the nutritional value.

SUMMARY
- One glaring difference between Coke and Pepsi is in the sodium levels listed on the nutrition panel. Coke contains 25mg of sodium per 250ml serve compared to Pepsi's 8.8mg.
- Both are extremely high in sugar at about 5 tsp per 250ml.
- The caramel IV colouring used in both is highly controversial. See my analysis of Zooper Dooper Flavoured Ice Confection Mix in Chapter Nine.

Vitafresh Raspberry Drink Vs Raspberry Flavoured Soft Drink

If you're looking for a red, raspberry flavoured drink for your kids on a hot summer's day, then I would always recommend going for the one with no artificial flavours, colours or preservatives, which is the Vitafresh. It is also lower in kilojoules (223 compared with 350) and has added vitamin C. I'm not very happy with the use of caramel IV which has question marks hanging over it (see "Coke vs Pepsi") but you can buy the same product without added colour and the rest of the ingredients stack up well for healthy eaters. It is interesting that both products "pump up" the sweetness by adding sweeteners — natural in the case of Vitafresh and artificial for the raspberry flavoured soft drink. Vitafresh also comes in cheaper (if you don't count the cost of tap water) at $2.59 for five litres compared to $3.88 for five litres of the Raspberry drink.

SUMMARY
- Both "pump up" the sweetness of the drinks by supplementing the sugar with sweeteners.
- Both have less sugar per 200ml than orange juice.
- One uses nothing artificial and the other uses artificial flavour, colour, sweetener and preservative.

Powerade — Mountain Blast — 750ml

The fine print on this label says "drink 250ml every 15 minutes during sustained strenuous exercise" which clearly implies that this isn't something you drink on your way to school or when you're not exercising. Most health experts recommend that water is the ideal hydration fuel for light or moderate exercise of fewer than 60 minutes. Drinking sports drinks without working off the energy can lead to weight gain in children. So if you have an extremely active athletic child you will need to look at hydrating them with extra measures, but perhaps finding a source without artificial flavours or colours would be better for them. You could also purchase the sports drinks powders which are available and make them up at half strength to reduce sugar levels.

SUMMARY
- Uses artificial colour and flavour.
- 10.7 tsp of sugar and 12g of maltodextrin per bottle.
- Designed for extreme athletes, not for your kid walking to school.

Sugar Levels

Coke and Pepsi — about 5 tsp per 250ml.
Monster Energy — 6 tsp per 250ml.
Powerade — a little more than 3 tsp per 250ml.
Vitafresh Raspberry Drink — 3 tsp per 200ml (topped up with artificial sweetener).
Raspberry Flavoured Soft Drink — nearly 4 tsp per 200ml (topped up with artificial sweetener).

— my recipes —

Lemon/Lime Water

This tastes a lot like the flavoured waters you can buy and really quenches your thirst.

>½ tsp citric acid
>4 tsp sugar
>Juice of 1 lime or lemon

Add these ingredients to 1 litre of ice cold water, then slice up the squeezed lemon or lime and throw in as well. Great for the morning after the night before!

Time taken: 5 minutes.

Lemon Barley Water

This uses honey instead of sugar. It takes less honey to achieve a sweet taste. Honey is absorbed into the body more slowly than sugar, so it has a lower glycemic index and it has many beneficial vitamins and minerals, unlike sugar which has little nutritional value.

This was given to invalids in the old days and is also a treatment for sore throats and cystitis in women. This would be a wonderful drink in hot months or if you are bit under the weather.

¾ cup of pearl barley

Finely grated zest and juice of 2 lemons

½ cup of honey

1 ½ litres of water

Place the barley in a sieve and rinse under cold water until water runs clear. Place in a saucepan with grated lemon zest and 6 cups of water. Bring to the boil over medium heat. Once boiling, simmer for 10 minutes then strain mixture into a heatproof bowl. Discard the barley (you can add it to a casserole or soup if you like). Add honey to bowl and stir to dissolve. Stir in lemon juice and then let mixture cool to room temperature. Pour into a lovely old jug and keep in the fridge.

Time taken: 20 minutes.

Sun Tea

>4 herbal tea bags (I use fruit or berry mixes)
>1 litre of water

Find a glass jar (not plastic as it may leach chemicals in the sun). Place four fruity teabags into the jar — they need to be very fruity. Pour on water and then sit it in the hot sun. It will gradually take on a bright pink colour and the tea will have steeped. Bring inside, store in the fridge and serve over lots of ice and a slice of lemon. If you have a sweet tooth, add some sugar or stevia.

Time taken: 5 minutes plus sun time.

Iced Tea

>4 tea bags (I use Dilmah)
>2 Healtheries Lemon and Lemongrass tea bags

Put in a jug and add 5 cups of water. Sit the jug in the sun for 30 minutes and then squeeze out tea bags and put the jug in the fridge. If you are in a hurry, use boiling water and steep for 5 minutes before removing bags and letting cool.

Time taken: 5 minutes plus sun time.

Easy Ginger Beer

My Dad used to make ginger beer and at the time it seemed like a very long and involved process. I haven't tried to make it his way but this is a very quick and easy way to make it and there's not too much sugar in it.

140g fresh ginger root
4 tbsp brown sugar
3 lemons
1 litre soda water or sparkling water

Leave the skin on your ginger roots and grate as best you can. Put the ginger and any juice into a large jug and add the sugar and the rind of your lemons. Mash it all about a bit with the end of a rolling pin, and then pour on the sparkling water and the juice from the lemons. Pour through a muslin cloth or similar to get rid of the ginger bits and then serve with ice.

If it is too sour add sugar and if it is too sweet add more lemon juice.

Time taken: 15 minutes.

CONCLUSIONS
- Nana never drank soft drinks, so why do we?
- Soft drinks are believed to be the main reason we consume much more sugar than we used to.
- Too much sugar leads to obesity, diabetes and other diseases.
- The acidity of soft drinks can affect the enamel of our teeth.
- Children who drink soft drinks consume less milk and fruit juice, which are good for them.
- Drinking diet drinks won't solve the problem.
- Water is, and always will be, the best thing to drink.

CHAPTER ELEVEN

sugar

how sweet it was

In our house we will often run out of sugar and we won't notice until someone comes around for a cup of coffee or tea.

"Milk or sugar?" I'll ask.

"White and two," they'll say.

Which is when I go rifling through the pantry trying to find some and end up scraping the last remaining grains out of the sugar bowl, and hoping they don't notice.

Unless someone's been baking or making jam there is no call for sugar in our house. Once Alex and Daniel (our sweet-tooths) left home we found we just didn't use it.

"I don't have a single sweet tooth," I said to Paul confidently one day as I was preparing to interview Australian author David Gillespie, who lost 40kg by giving up sugar — which he calls "sweet poison". He has written a book on the subject called *Big, Fat, Lies*. "I should be as thin as a bean if everything he says is true!"

"I've got one word for you," said Paul. "Wine."

Indeed. Alcohol is basically fermented sugar, so

I was probably consuming quite a bit with my frequent glasses of sauvignon blanc.

And so, I put it to David live on air the next day.

"Is wine full of sugar?"

His reply left me eager to get home and take the rare opportunity to prove Paul wrong.

"A dry white wine contains barely any sugar, because it is converted into alcohol. A sweet wine, on the other hand, still has some in there."

What a relief. I need to point out, however, that the calories in a 150ml glass of dry white wine add up to about 100, so it's still worth cutting it out if you're trying to lose weight.

Meanwhile outside our house, in the real world, sugar continues to be linked to numerous health problems including obesity and diabetes. In this country 50 people are diagnosed with diabetes a day.

The *New Zealand Medical Journal* estimates that we eat 138g of sugar a day or 32 teaspoons (1 teaspoon of sugar equals 4.2g). When you look at this amount it seems incredible that you would physically go and spoon 32 teaspoons of sugar out of a jar and eat it every day. But the problem with our sugar problem is that most of it is hidden in our food without us realising it. I call it "suppressed sugar" because just like in a court case, where a defendant has their name suppressed so that the media can't identify them, the sugar is in food but it essentially has its name suppressed unless you go looking for it.

In Nana's day there was sugar in baking, preserves, jams, puddings and cordials. But she didn't go to the supermarket and bring home food which had "invisible" sugar added to it.

Probably the first instance of suppressed sugar I noticed was when McDonald's started up in New Zealand and their hamburger buns tasted unbearably sweet to me. But as a nation we got used to it.

Then we started drinking more and more soda drinks, which, as you know from Chapter 10, are laden with sugar.

Today I still get a surprise when I bite into a product from the supermarket which is supposed to be savoury — like some crackers Paul brought home just the other night -and find out it is incredibly sweet and turns out to have lots of sugar in it.

Anyone who has read books by Michael Pollan will know that in the US there was a very sinister reason for sugar to be put in practically every food the Americans ate. The country had a huge corn glut which was bringing down the price of grain, so corn and its by-product high fructose corn syrup, which is very similar to sugar, was fed to their animals and put in their food and drinks to use it up.

We don't have that problem in New Zealand but we do have marketing campaigns which tell our kids it's cool to drink Coke or Powerade. We have marketing to encourage our kids to eat junk food. It is now so cheap that picking up a meal from McDonald's or KFC is no longer a luxury. Most processed food will have sugar in it to help it taste good.

During our interview, David Gillespie explained to me that there were sugars that were important for our diet as well as the bad ones. The important sugars are glucose, which is found in all food, galactose which is in very small quantities in dairy products, and fructose, which is found in ripe fruits.

What we don't need is sucrose, which we know as "table sugar". The reason table sugar is bad for us is that it is empty calories with no nutritional benefit whatsoever. It is also highly addictive and it can cause many diseases. If you don't believe me, try typing "sucrose is good for you" into Google and see how you get on.

WHEN I WAS a child my mother was an expert on finding foods which would help you lose weight. For years she drank Tab, which was an ultra-feminine drink in a bright pink can which had no calories and loads of artificial sweetener in it. There was always saccharin in abundance, and we were encouraged to use it instead of sugar.

Which wasn't so much of a problem for me, because I didn't use sugar and besides I never liked the bitter aftertaste of saccharin.

But my brother, Mark, went for it big time. He replaced the six teaspoons of sugar he would have on his Weet-bix with saccharin and put it in his tea and coffee.

After a while we noticed some quite unsightly wart-like growths emerging on his hands. I'm not sure who told him to lay off the artificial sweeteners, but he did and the growths disappeared. I pinpoint this moment when I was only about eight-years-old as my first realisation that food made in laboratories might not be good for you.

Saccharin has largely been replaced by aspartame

in many foods, because many studies on animals showed that it can cause cancer and increase the potency of other cancer-causing chemicals. In 1977 the American Food and Drug Association asked for it to be banned, but they were unsuccessful. However, products containing saccharin were required to have a warning notice printed on their labels. In 1997, the diet-food industry lobbied to get that removed, and in 2000 saccharin was removed from the government list of cancer-causing chemicals and late that year the requirement for a warning notice on labels was lifted.

Many people, like me, still avoid it, convinced that those original studies have much more weight than the lobbying powers of the extremely well-funded weight-loss industry.

My parents, however, have continued to use artificial sweeteners, particularly my father in his coffee and tea.

Two years ago, after he was diagnosed with bowel cancer, and had a tumour removed, I went over with all my books and tried to talk to him and my mother about processed food, and getting back to real food. I talked at length about artificial sweeteners. If I had my way I would have had them planting an organic garden full of brassicas, eating nothing but raw wholefoods, getting rid of a lot of dairy from their diet and embarking on a cancer-free way of living.

But in reality, my parents generally eat a really good, healthy diet. They cook fresh meat and fish and eat lots of veges every day, but my dad loves to use his sweeteners.

I suggested that perhaps he could try a new product I had found called stevia, which is a South American plant which looks a bit like mint and whose leaves are very sweet. (That's the plant on the lovely painting which opened this chapter.) You can now get it powdered and in tablets so that you can add it to your tea or coffee.

Something must have got through, because Dad asked me to get him some and that is what he now uses. He still won't eat yoghurt, however, which I spoon-fed him after his operation, to counteract the effects of all the antibiotics he was on after he picked up a nasty infection at the hospital.

"I'm not eating that," he said horrified.

"I've got the one with honey in it and lots of beneficial bacteria, it will taste fine," I cajoled.

"Just a spoonful then."

You would have thought I was attempting to feed him fish guts, the look on his face was so horrified. Actually I think he would have preferred me to feed him fish guts. He's a keen fisherman.

But now Dad's cancer has gone and I'm confident my parents will both live to a ripe old age, free of artificial sweeteners.

Stevia does seem too good to be true. It's completely plant-based and is about 300 times sweeter than sugar, but with no calories. I have a plant growing in my garden and if I want to sweeten something like a cocoa or a masala chai tea, then I'll break off a leaf and throw it in.

However, some people are not too sure. The Japanese have been using it for years but any new food needs rigorous testing. People at the Center for Science in the Public Interest say that if you're going to have it in your tea and coffee a couple of times a day, then it is probably fine. But they worry that, as with anything in America, it will become saturated through the soft drink market the minute Coke and Pepsi get their hands on it. And like anything, too much is not a good thing.

Another concern is that its good name is being abused, because products might indeed contain stevia, but they will also contain other artificial sweeteners which aren't so safe. In this country I've seen products which combine stevia with erythritol, which is a naturally occurring sugar alcohol

So if, like me, you like to use it occasionally as an alternative to sugar, go for it. We'll wait and see what happens to Americans if it turns up in their sodas.

There are some artificial sweeteners I would never recommend giving to your children or eating yourself and it is surprising how often they pop up.

I analysed a common chewing gum called Mentos Aqua Kiss 3D Sugarfree Gum. In it I found eight sweeteners, two of which have health queries associated with them, not to mention a colour banned in other countries and an anti-oxidant listed as a carcinogen in California.

All this in one innocent packet of chewing gum, picked up by your child on the way to school.

Sugarfree gum enjoys high status because dentists everywhere will tell you that it's good not to have sugar near the teeth, but what are we putting in our children's mouths instead?

I think the best approach with kids is to treat anything sweet as a treat food, not something we consume daily as part of our regular diet. Simply replacing sugar-laden foods like sweets and soft drinks with "diet" versions laced with chemicals is not a good solution.

The trick is to get your sugar buzz from fruits and foods where you can see the sugar because you sprinkled it on or used it in baking. And to be ever vigilant for suppressed sugar in the foods you bring home from the supermarket or junk food outlets.

My Findings:
Artificial Sweeteners to Avoid

Artificial sweeteners don't break down in our bodies, nor do wastewater-treatment plants catch them before they enter waterways, researchers have found. In 2009, Swiss scientists tested water samples from wastewater-treatment plants, rivers and lakes in Switzerland and detected levels of acesulfame K, sucralose, and saccharin, all of which are, or have been, used in diet sodas. A recent test of 19 municipal water supplies in the US revealed the presence of sucralose in every one. It's not clear yet what these low levels are doing to people, but research has found that sucralose in rivers and lakes interferes with some organisms' feeding habits.

Acesulfame K

This is acesulphame potassium, which is a chemical that is 200 times sweeter than sugar. Its approval for use in 1988 was controversial as the Center for Science in the Public Interest, a Washington consumer group, said that animals fed this in two different studies suffered more tumours than others that did not receive the compound. The FDA (Food and Drug Administration) said that four long-term animal studies in dogs, mice and rats had not shown any toxic effects and approved its use.

Aspartame

This artificial sweetener has had a very controversial ride in the food industry. Otherwise known as NutraSweet it is a compound prepared from aspartic acid and phenylalanine which is about 200 times sweeter than sugar. There have been objections made that it might cause brain damage and that when used in soft drinks it deteriorates into toxic levels of methyl alcohol under storage conditions. Neither claim was accepted, and it has been approved as a sweetener since 1981. However aspartame must be avoided by people with the genetic condition phenylketonuria or PKU which means a person cannot break down phenylalanine which is an ingredient in aspartame.

Saccharin

In 1977 the American Food and Drug Association asked for this to be banned because of concerns it caused cancer in animal studies, but they were unsuccessful. However products containing saccharin were required to have a warning notice printed on their labels. This requirement has since been removed.

Cyclamate

This controversial high-potency sweetener was used in the United States in diet foods until 1970, at which time it was banned. However, it is still used in many products in New Zealand. Animal studies indicated that it caused cancer. Now, based on animal studies, it is believed not to cause cancer directly, but to increase the potency of other carcinogens and to harm the testes.

— *my alternative sweeteners* —

Honey

Honey is a good alternative to sugar as it takes less of it to achieve a sweet taste. It is absorbed into the body more slowly than sugar, so it has a lower GI, and it has many beneficial vitamins and minerals, unlike sugar, which has little nutritional value. It also has anti-microbial properties.

Stevia

A herb native to South America, stevia is 300 times sweeter than sugar. It has been used as a sweetener for centuries in South America, and in Japan it makes up 41 per cent of the sweetener market. Stevia has no calories and no glycemic impact, making it suitable for diabetics as well as weight watchers.

Xylitol

Xylitol is a five-carbon sugar (five carbon atoms in the molecule) unlike most other sugars, which have six. This subtle difference means it helps prevent the growth of bacteria, so doesn't ferment in the mouth as sugar does. So it is mostly used in chewing gums.

Brown Rice Syrup

Made from boiling brown rice, the syrup is gluten- and wheat-free. More suitable for cooking than adding to tea, it can also be used as a condiment and drizzled over pancakes or porridge. It has a slightly butterscotch flavour.

Barley Malt Syrup

Similar to molasses in texture, barley malt syrup has, unsurprisingly, a malty taste. This makes it ideal for baking in bread. It's also easily digested and has a low glycemic index.

Coconut Sugar

Coconuts are very trendy at the moment. This sugar is taken from the sap of the coconut palm. It is nutritious and has a low score on the glycemic index. It tastes similar to brown sugar, but is slightly richer.

Date Sugar

This is made from dehydrated dates, which are ground to produce the sugar. Retaining many of the nutritional benefits of dates, it has a rich sweet flavour that makes it an ideal alternative to brown sugar. Unfortunately it doesn't melt and is difficult to dissolve, making it unsuitable for use in drinks and some baking.

Maple Syrup

Maple syrup can be used in place of sugar and it has a very distinctive taste. You can also get maple sugar, which is made from dehydrated maple syrup. Like coconut sugar, it can replace regular sugar, as and when you need it.

Molasses

This is a by-product of the sugar production process. Because of the way table sugar is produced, many of the nutritional benefits are left in the molasses. Blackstrap molasses is a good source of iron and calcium. It's quite thick and viscous and is best used in baking. It is sweeter than sugar, so you'll need less.

CONCLUSIONS

- New Zealanders eat an average of 32 teaspoons of sugar a day.
- Sugar is an empty food, because it provides no nutrition in return for high calories.
- "Suppressed sugar" is in many foods, including savoury foods.
- Stevia is a good alternative to sugar, if you need a no-calorie option.
- Learning to get sweetness from natural foods such as fruit is a good idea.
- Replacing sweet foods with "diet" versions doesn't deal with the sugar addiction.
- Some artificial sweeteners have terrible health studies attached to them and should be avoided.
- There are many natural sugar alternatives which provide good nutrition, such as honey and molasses.

conclusion

eat don't diet

I'm a size 16, which I have been since about a week after I met Paul in 1995. When I met him I was size 14, but then he fed me gourmet meals which he cooked just for me and I insisted he keep doing it. Before that I was a size 12, until I had children.

Over the years, I've tried everything everyone has tried. Weightwatchers, Jenny Craig, those disgusting milk shake things you buy at the chemist, herbal supplements, liver cleansing and one year I kept a food diary of everything I ate. I lost five kilos and as soon as I stopped the diary I put them back on again.

This year I've opted for eating more vegetables and continuing to reject any food which has more than five ingredients on the label. Instead of Meat-Free Mondays, I have Meaty Mondays, only eating meat once a week.

I also went back to the gym and started swimming again, because I realised what few muscles my body possessed had gone into retirement.

It wasn't a weight-loss thing, more a healthy

thing. Everyone knows eating more vegetables and fruit is good for you. But secretly, as I munched through yet another delicious beetroot salad, I was hoping that after a few months my body would have an "Aha!" moment and reward me with some weight loss.

"This is what I've been wanting all along," it would say to me. "Miraculously I am finally in balance and you are one of those people who, when people comment on your new size, can frustratingly say: 'It just happened!'"

I would look at my friends who do months of strict non-drinking, exercising three hours a day, eating nothing diets and lose loads of weight and say "Neh, not for me. Real food, vegetables and exercise is all I need!"

When I did public speaking in future, I would hold up a picture of me at size 16 and reveal my secret. "Real food, vegetables and exercise!" And everyone would give me a standing ovation.

And along with the more vegetables, I decided to give myself a break.

"You are who you are, and you are about to turn 50, so just accept yourself and get on with worrying about big things in life, like child poverty and cruelty to animals."

It was all going quite well until I played back a television piece I had done on *Good Morning*, when I had taken in my hen Olive to talk about how to keep chickens in the urban environment.

As I looked at the close-up of Olive looking very gorgeous I thought to myself: "I can't remember there being a cushion behind Olive."

And that the cushion was brown, the same colour as the top I was wearing, and that cushion was my stomach.

"Arghhh!" I screamed and haven't played back any more *Good Morning* pieces since.

THE ONE MISTAKE you must never make when you embark on changing your diet to include real foods only, is believing that you will lose weight.

I'm still stubbornly the same size 16 I have been for years. And I think the words "home," "made" and "sourdough" might have something to do with it.

The reality is that by eating healthier food you are getting a lot more nutrition, so you actually don't have to eat as much.

There is a theory that our bodies are hardwired to search out and consume the things we need in food. So, if we need some vitamin C, we'll find ourselves craving an orange; or if we need some zinc we'll want oysters. I believe that this was once the case when we still possessed the ability to "listen to our bodies" as yoga teachers like to say.

These days I think our appetite is governed more by how something looks or smells. And the fact that after we eat a Big Mac we are still hungry could well be because there wasn't a lot of nutrition in it and we are simply needing more vitamins, minerals and fatty acids. Or it could be that we're just greedy.

While I was writing this book, I took a few weeks off to go to India. I say that like I was taking a holiday to somewhere exotic, but in reality it was three of the hardest weeks of my life. India is chaotic and confronting, often unsettling, frequently amazing, and finally awe-inspiring. Paul and I escorted a tour there and we were really busy getting 14 people on and off buses, planes and trains and into hotels, while the unfettered chaos that is everyday Indian life went on around us.

But we had a lot of long bus trips, and that was when I watched with interest the lives of the Indian people, both in the cities and in the rural areas. To be honest it was medieval. Not a lot had changed in their lives since the Middle Ages except perhaps the advent of the car horn, which I think Indians value more than the actual car for its ability to make a loud noise as often and frequently as possible.

Back here in New Zealand, I've been writing books and going on the radio harping on about the need to live a life more like our Nanas' — a mere 80 to 100 years ago.

These people are living a life more like their ancestors did centuries ago. And what I noticed most was the food. Dhal, curries, naan bread made on the side of the road, samosas, bhaji, pakora. Not a lot of meat, lots of wholegrains and acres of vegetables and fruit.

A wonderfully healthy diet, I thought to myself and then I was struck by something which was becoming as common a sight as beggar children and chai wallahs.

Small bowls. It didn't matter if I was on a rickshaw making my way through a crowded bazaar in Varanasi, in the old town of Delhi or out in the relative peace and quiet of a little village in Uttarakhand near the jungle. Men would huddle in a street stall shovelling food out of a bowl not much bigger than a coffee mug at lunchtime. Women who had spent the morning harvesting wheat in 38°C heat would huddle under the shade of trees and eat from similar-sized bowls. And later in the day, there were those bowls again, feeding people for dinner. Just one small bowl with all their food for that meal in it.

Yes, there is fried food, but I never saw anyone eating from a plate piled high with the stuff, as you would see in New Zealand.

This had a huge effect on me, as I mentally calculated how many calories these people were living on each day, and it came in at about 2000 tops, if that. I wasn't far out. When I got home, I found an article in *The Hindu* (my favourite newspaper while I was over there) which said that the average daily calorie intake for an Indian in a rural area was 2020 and in an urban area 1946 in 2009–2010. This was not seen as good news by the paper, as it was lower than previous years, despite India enjoying good economic growth.

It soon became very easy to see where that economic growth was showing, and that was on the waistlines of the Indians who were staying in the same hotels as us. They were plump and proud, carrying with them all the accoutrements and surly attitudes of the newly rich we have become used to in the West.

When it comes to keeping healthy I have learned many things during my years of research, writing and harping on. These are what I know to be facts:
- Eating a diet of real food, similar to the one your Nana ate, is much healthier for you than eating processed foods found in the supermarkets.
- The fewer ingredients a processed food has, the better it is for you.
- Eating fresh food, bought locally or grown yourself is more nutritious than stuff which has been lying around in supermarkets for days, weeks and months.
- If you eat a heavily nutritious diet of real food, you are less likely to eat too much. If you eat nutrition-less junk food you will need to eat more of it to get the nutrients you need.
- You cannot trust the government or the supermarket owners to have your family's best health interests at the forefront of their decision-making.
- You need to protect your children from toxins in food by reading ingredients labels closely because no one else will.
- Home-made food has no additives or chemicals.
- Alcohol is gorgeous, especially when you get to the end of writing a book, but it is high in calories and offers no nutrition.

As a result of living a life using these facts (well not always the alcohol one) the benefits have been subtle (no weight-loss) but noticeable all the same. Our family rarely gets sick anymore. Gone are the days when the whole family would come down with a flu or stomach bug which would hang around for weeks. This could be because we have got rid of all the chemical cleaners from our house and use our natural cleaning products, but I think it is also because we are giving our bodies a much better chance of fighting back by feeding them well and giving them the nutrients to fend off disease.

I prefer to believe that bugs don't cause illness; it's how our bodies react to the bugs that makes you ill. That is why two people can be exposed to the same flu or diarrhoea bug but only one gets sick with it. And why when you are run down, not eating properly, stressed or drinking too much you'll get sick, but when you are exercising and eating properly you rarely get struck down. The bugs are in us all the time — it's how good our body is at fighting them that matters. And your body fights better when it is fed properly.

I like the analogy used by Allan Carr in his book *Easy Way to Lose Weight*. He says if your car ran out of petrol and you didn't have access to any you could reason that plastic bags would do because they are made from the same stuff as petrol. But if you stuffed your car with plastic bags it just wouldn't work.

Our bodies are the same. They are designed to eat real food and have been eating real food for thousands of years, just like the Indians do. Taking something which resembles real food, such as a liquid full of chemicals which tastes like tomato soup but isn't, will have the same result. And he points out that it's interesting how well we treat our cars, which we can replace if they break down, but we only have one body, for a lifetime.

SO THAT JUST leaves portion size. Do we really need that much food? My problem has always been that I think it is the ultimate insult to someone if you leave food on your plate. This was taught to me by my parents, along with other important table manners like putting your knife and fork down between mouthfuls, not leaning on your elbows at the table and closing your mouth when you chew. I was also taught that it is very embarrassing and rather uncouth to ask to take home food at a restaurant. Something I could never do until our daughter Pearl taught me that it is perfectly okay.

We were in New York together for 10 days while I worked, and every night we would go out to dinner and she would eat only a third to a half of her meal. Pearl never over-eats, probably because, unlike my parents, we never made her eat all her dinner before she got dessert. If she'd had enough, that was fine.

Each time she cheerily asked to take it home and her waiter or waitress equally cheerily took it off and wrapped it up for her.

So simple.

So I can add another food fact to my list and that is: "Eat like an Indian."

I HOPE YOU have enjoyed reading this book and that you will make use of the food code guide on the next pages and the lovely eggs which are designed as an easy guide to check which additives to avoid while you are shopping. I like to think that when this book has been on sale for a while, I'll be in my local supermarket and I'll see people reach into their handbags or backpacks and bring out this book to have a look at those eggs to check they are bringing home good food.

I also hope that you will join the unofficial movement many other New Zealanders — and I — have joined, which is to use our consumer power and reject bad food, rejoice and support good food and its producers and, most importantly, protect our families from Big Food.

And finally to quote the man who inspired me to become the food bore I am today, Michael Pollan: "Eat food, not too much, mostly plants."

acknowledgements

None of my books would happen without the amazing feedback I get every day by email from the readers of my newsletter and columns, Facebook and Twitter followers and radio listeners. Thank you to everyone who has contributed ideas such as this book and its name, shared their own experiences about keeping chickens or living like their Nana, or just written to say, "Keep up the good work." I would be nowhere without you.

Thanks also to our daughter, Alex Scott, for being such a wonderfully talented artist and agreeing to take on the huge amount of work involved in painting the wonderful cover and illustrations. And to our designer, Katy Yiakmis, who, as always, understood the book immediately and produced it so well. I've never had such a pretty book.

Also a big thank you to Tim Murphy, Shayne Currie and David Hastings, my bosses at the *New Zealand Herald* for believing in my column "Wendyl Wants to Know" and paying me to write it! And for letting me use some of the material from that column in this book. Also thanks to Sarah Stuart, the editor of *NZ Woman's Weekly* for letting me reproduce some of the recipes from my "Nana's Pantry" column. And to Bryce Johns, the editor of the *Herald on Sunday* for letting me adapt some of my columns from his newspaper.

Thanks to my gorgeous children and grandchildren — all seven of you - for once again allowing me to include you in my stories. To my parents Cedric and Elis Nissen for accepting my versions of childhood events. And to my good friend, Kerre Woodham, for giving wine and sympathy when I struggled to meet my deadline, as usual, and providing the kind of support that only other writers can.

And finally to my husband, Paul Little, who edits my books with patience, listens to his wife with understanding and supports me in everything I do.

further reading

These are the books I have read and enjoyed and you might too. Some are lovely cookbooks and others write well about food and the food industry.

Additive Alert: Your Guide to Safer Shopping, Julie Eady, www.additivealert.com.au.

A Consumer's Dictionary of Food Additives, Ruth Winter, M.S, Three Rivers Press, 2004

Animal, Vegetable, Miracle: a year of food life, Barbara Kingsolver, Faber and Faber, 2008

An Everlasting Meal: cooking with economy and grace, Tamar Adler, Scribner, 2011

Appetite for Profit: How the food industry undermines our health and how to fight back, Michele Simon, Nation Books, 2008

Big, Fat, Lies: how the diet industry is making you sick, fat & poor, David Gillespie, Penguin, 2012

Chez Panisse Vegetables, Alice Waters, Harper Collins, 1996

Eat Smart, Stay Well, Susanna Lyle, David Bateman, 2010

Fast Food Nation, Eric Schlosser, Penguin, 2002

Food Rules: an eater's manual, Michael Pollan, Penguin, 2010

Healing with Whole Foods: Asian traditions and modern nutrition,
  Paul Pitchford, North Atlantic Books, 2003
In Defence of Food: an eater's manifesto, Michael Pollan,
  Penguin, 2009
*Nourishing Traditions: the cookbook that challenges politically
  correct nutrition and the diet dictocrats*, Sally Fallon. New
  Trends Publishing, 1999
River Cottage Veg Everyday!, Hugh Fearnley-Whittingstall,
  Bloomsbury, 2011
*Slow Death by Rubber Duck: How the toxic chemistry of everyday
  life affects our health*, Rick Smith/Bruce Lourie,
  University of Queensland Press.
The China Study, T. Colin Campbell, PhD and Thomas
  M. Campbell II, MD, Benbella Books, 2006
The Omnivore's Dilemma: a natural history of four meals,
  Michael Pollan, Penguin, 2006
The Self Health Revoltuion, J. Michael Zenn.
We want real food: the local food lover's bible, Graham Harvey,
  Robinson, 2008.

To read more of the Wendyl Wants to Know columns
in the Weekend Herald go to:
http://tiny.cc/0Ib9u

praise for other books by Wendyl Nissen

BITCH AND FAMOUS

I have to say I really genuinely loved this book and I really didn't expect to. I expected to gag at her bitchiness and shallowness and be irritated by an endless parade of pseudo macho conflict driven encounters by people who are famous only for being famous. There's a bit of all that but Wendyl's writing is so good and her personal insights so raw and honest that one simply can't help responding to her as a human and not just the bitch of the title... Often crass, always outspoken she is a woman of outrageous cheek and unusual sensibility and intelligence. I strongly recommend picking up a copy of Bitch and Famous.

—Margie Thomson, Easymix

"Extremely enjoyable, extremely entertaining...a fascinating insight."
—Paul Holmes, NewstalkZB.

This book is only available from wendylsgreengoddess.co.nz

Domestic Goddess on a Budget

"Absolutely brilliant, this handy little book will become a household bible for beautifying your house and person in the greenest possible way...we suspect that using this book could be as good for the soul as for our bodies and the planet."
—Margie Thomson, NEXT magazine.

"A great sort of book to flick through and see what tips you can find — I've had it sitting on my coffee table and I think everyone who's been around has picked it up."
—Kelly Clark, Greymouth Evening Star

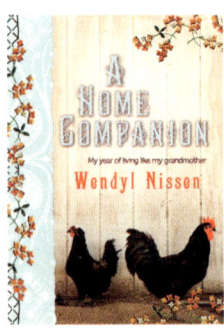

A Home Companion — My Year of Living Like My Grandmother.

"It's okay to be a nana," says the once tough-as-painted-nails media mover and shaker Wendyl Nissen. Written in an easy-to-read, humorous style, with a sprinkling of handy tips. A Home Companion is the ideal bedside book to dip into."
—Sarah Heeringa, GOOD magazine.

"This is a charming, easy read: Part memoir, part home-making guide, part manifesto for a healther life."
Eleanor Black, NEXT magazine.

Mother's Little Helper — an old-fashioned guide to raising your baby chemical-free.

"Her honesty and humour is clearly heard in her words. I wish I had this book to read during my first pregnancy. What a wealth of vital information for all new mums."
—Lorraine Downes

"This wonderful book is the perfect gift for new mums. Packed full of sensible advice and common sense, it's like having a grandmother on hand at any hour of the day and night."
—Kerre Woodham

"What a thoroughly useful, sensible and reassuring source of information for new mums . . . I'm certainly going to make sure my daughter has a copy!"
—Judy Bailey

All Wendyl's books are available for sale on WWW.WENDYLSGREENGODDESS.CO.NZ

index

RECIPES

Additive-Free Noodles 187
Alex's Coconut Ice 235
Alex's Fudge 234
Alternative Sweeteners 269
Anchovy butter 100
Aromatic Turkey/Chicken in a Bag 190
Barley Sugars 237
Beef Stock 188
Best Wholemeal Bread 167
Berry Smoothie 139
Billy Bread 166
Bircher Muesli 137
Bob each way spread 101
Brandy butter 100
Butter 99
Cheese Biscuits 212
Cheese Crackers 212
Cheese and Salmon Paste 216
Chicken Nuggets 50
Chicken Stock 189
Chocolate Ganache 103
Crumpets 168
Curried Eggs 194
Dairy-free Pesto 120
Easy Ginger Beer 255
Easy White Bread 162
Ever Ready Paste 215
Fudge Cake 209
Green Smoothie 139
Guacamole 117
Herb butter 100
Hokey Pokey Biscuits 210
Home-made Bacon 51
Herbed Salt 52
Hummus 117
Ice Treats 234
Iced Tea 255
Lemon Barley Water 254
Lemon Fudge Fingers 209
Lemon/Lime Water 253
Low-Fat, Low-Sugar Toasted Muesli 136
Marinated Chicken Nibbles 51
Muesli Bars 213
Mum's Broken Biscuits (Uncooked) Orange Fudge 208
Nut Butter 119
Nuts and Raisins 217
Oat Cakes 74
Oat Fudge Squares 209
Oatie Smoothie 139
Old-Fashioned Granny

Peppermints 236
Onion Dip 117
Pea and Lemon Dip 118
Peanut Butter 119
Pita Bread 164
Pita chips 74
Pizza Bread 166
Pork & Thyme Sausages 49
Porridge 135
Potato chips 73
Potted Tomato Paste 214
Risotto 191
Roast Chicken 53
Roast lamb 54
Roast beef 54
Sardine Paste 215
Scalloped Sweet Corn 194
Smashed chickpea and Avocado Dip 118
Sourdough Bread 164
Strawberry Pineapple Smoothie 139
Sun Tea 255
Tomato Soup 187
Vegan Beetroot Chocolate Cake 102
Vegetarian Potted Meat 216
Weet-Bix Smoothjie 138
Welsh Rarebit 193
Yoghurt 101

ANALYSES

ACT II Butter Lover's Flavour Popcorn 72
Ajitsuke Nori (sea weed sacks) 72
Arnott's Shapes – Pizza 70
Arnott's Iced Animals 207
Arnott's Tiny Teddy Chocolate Biscuits 208
Artificial Sweeteners to Avoid 267
Bellisimo All Natural Chicken Arrabiata 185
Chop Chop! Chicken Chunks – Smoked Flavour 46
Coke 250
Collisions Mint Treats 206
Deli-Menu Fish Pie with Tuna 186
Dolmio Pasta Bake Tuna Bake Sauce 186
Fish Fingers – Independent Fisheries 43
Fresh 'n' Fruity Berries Galore Low Fat Yoghurt 98
Fruit Hitz 69
Hellers Free Farmed Country Pork Sausages 40
Home Brand Table Spread 97

Huttons Ham & Chicken Flavoured Luncheon Chub 42
Kellog's Froot Loops 134
Kiwi Dip – Nestle Reduced Cream and Maggi Onion Soup Mix 116
Kiwi Roast Lamb & Mint Shaved 45
Krispies 206
Le Snak Cheese 206
Milkies Choc Vanilla 206
Monster Energy 500 ml 249
MTR Alu Methi (potato and fenugreek curry) 185
Naked Panda Green Chicken Curry with Noodles 186
Nestle Milo Oats 133
Nice & Natural Nut Bar Original 207
Oki Doki Disco Bars 205
One Square Meal 205
Pepsi 250
Powerade Mountain Blast – 750 ml 252
Raspberry Jam Slice 205
Raspberry Flavoured Soft Drink 251
Ryvita Fruit and Seed Crunch with Honey 207
Signature Range Guacamole Creamy Dip 116
Sizzlers 39
Surimi Seafood Salad Mix 43
Tegel Crumbed Chicken Nuggets 41
Tip Top Super Soft White Sandwich 160
Twisties 71
Smooze 233
So Good Regular 98
The Natural Confectionery Co. Jelly Babies 233
Vitafresh Raspberry Drink 251
Vogel's Original Mixed Grain 160
Zooper Dooper Flavoured Ice Confection Mix – 8 Cosmic Flavours 229

how to read an ingredients label

This is my advice for how to read, and understand ingredients labels on processed foods:
- Invest in a magnifying glass.
- Keep a list (or this book) handy in your bag for easy reference for the worst ingredients to avoid.
- The ingredients will be listed in order of the greatest quantity. So if sugar is the first ingredient listed then there will be more sugar than any other ingredient in the food.
- The additive that is last on the list of ingredients will be present in the food in the smallest amount.
- "Flavours" or "Flavouring" means the flavour used in the product is artificial. If not it will state "Natural flavour" or "Nature-identical flavour." Natural flavour means it uses strawberries to make it taste like strawberries. A nature-identical flavour means that it might taste like strawberries but it's actually been made out of another natural product combination like apples and vinegar.
- If in doubt take it home and take your time. A big ingredients label takes time to analyse and if you end up not wanting to eat the food from your discoveries you can take it back.

nutrition label guidelines.

An easy way to tell if a food product is healthy is to follow these guidelines when looking at the per 100g column on the nutrition label.

Total Fat	less than 3g of total fat per 100g
Saturated fat	less than 1.5g of saturated fat per 100g
Sugar	less than 10g of sugar per 100g
Sodium	less than 300mg of sodium per 100g
Fibre	more than 3g fibre per serve (this is best judged per serve).

a guide to our food codes

There is no official food code guide which explains where the additives come from, what they do in food and whether they are any good for you. Our New Zealand Food Safety Authority has a booklet which tells you the name of the substance which corresponds to the code but no more. So on the net you will find many food code lists compiled from random people who do a quick search and happily repeat information which is not well researched or substantiated.

It was important to me that this guide was the most accurate I could compile so I used many sources including "A Consumer's Dictionary of Food Additives" by Ruth Winter, MS, the Center for Science in the Public Interest website, Wikipedia and some other sites I trusted. For every code I cross-referenced all the information from these sources in an effort to make my findings as accurate and informative as possible. You may find other sources claiming some of these additives are going to kill you, but I chose to take a cautious stance for this guide rather than an inflammatory one.

It is important that you use your own judgement when using the information provided in this guide.

You will notice that some numbers are missing from the list. This is because the additives are not allowed for use in foods that are sold in this country.

COLOURS

No.	Name	Comments
100	Curcumin/ Turmeric	Orange-yellow colour, derived from turmeric.
101	Riboflavin (vitamin B2)	Yellow colour.
102	Tartrazine	Yellow colour, banned in Norway and phased out in the UK. Can aggravate asthmatics and also cause migraine, blurred vision, itching, rhinitis and purple skin patches. In conjunction with Benzoic acid (E210) tartrazine appears to create an over-activity in children.
104	Quinoline yellow	Yellow colour, banned in US, Japan and Norway and phased out in the UK. Linked to hyperactivity, skin rashes. Asthmatics should avoid this.
110	Sunset yellow	Yellow colour, banned in Norway, Finland, largely phased out in the UK. Side effects can be urticaria (hives), rhinitis (runny nose), nasal congestion, allergies, hyperactivity, kidney tumours, chromosomal damage, abdominal pain, nausea and vomiting, indigestion, distaste for food; increased incidence of tumours in animals.
120	Cochineal, Carmine	Red colour, made from insects. Can cause hyperactivity.
122	Azorubine or Carmoisine	Red colour, banned in Sweden, US, Canada, Japan and Norway, phased out in the UK. Can cause allergic and/or intolerance reactions, particularly amongst those with an aspirin intolerance. Other reactions can include a rash similar to nettle rash and water retention.
123	Amaranth	Purple colour, banned in the United States in 1976, Russia, Norway and Austria, restricted in France and Italy. Can cause rash similar to nettle rash, particularly amongst those with an aspirin intolerance or asthmatics. Can provoke asthma, eczema and hyperactivity; it caused birth defects and foetal deaths in some animal tests.
124	Ponceau 4R	Red colour, phased out in the UK. Can cause allergic and/or intolerance reactions particularly amongst those with an aspirin intolerance or asthmatics. Carcinogen in animals.

127	Erythrosine	Red colour, banned in Norway and the US. There are fears that it could affect thyroid activity, can increase thyroid hormone levels, was shown to cause thyroid cancer in rats in a study in 1990.
129	Allura red AC	Red colour, banned in Denmark, Belgium, France and Switzerland, phased out in the UK. May have slightly less allergy/intolerance reaction by aspirin intolerant people and asthmatics than most of the azo dyes, although those with skin sensitivities should be careful. Allura red has also been connected with cancer in mice
132	Indigotine	Blue colour, banned in Norway. May cause nausea, vomiting, high blood pressure, skin rashes, breathing problems and other allergic reactions.
133	Brilliant blue FCF	Blue colour, banned in Argentina, Bulgaria, Czech Republic, France, Hungary, Mauritius, Morocco, Poland, Portugal, Trinidad and Turkey. Can cause allergic reactions in asthmatics.
140	Chlorophyll	Green to olive colour, no adverse effects are known.
141	Chlorophyll copper complexes	Olive colour, no adverse effects are known
142	Green S	Green colour, banned in the US, Sweden, Norway, Canada and Japan. Known to cause hyperactivity, asthma, uticaria (hives), and insomnia.
143	Fast Green FCF	Green colour. Causes tumours in animals.
150a	Caramel I	Dark brown colour, safest of the caramel colours. No ammonium or sulphites used in its production.
150b	Caramel II	Dark brown colour. Made by heating sugars with a sulphite.
150c	Caramel III	Dark brown colour. Made by heating sugars with ammonia.
150d	Caramel IV	Dark brown colour commonly used in beverages like Coke and even malt vinegar. Made by reacting corn sugar with ammonia and sulphites under high pressures and high temperatures. Those reactions produce the chemicals 2- methylimidazole and 4-methylimidazole (4-MEI). There is concern that 4-MEI is a carcinogen after tests on rats, however it is allowed in our food products.
151	Brilliant black BN	Black colour, banned in Denmark, Austria, Belgium, Canada, Finland, France, Germany, Japan, Norway, Switzerland, Sweden, US.

153	Carbon black	Black colour, banned in the United States in 1976 due to concerns it was a carcinogen.
155	Brown HT	Brown colour, banned in Austria, Belgium, Denmark, France, Germany, Norway, Sweden, Switzerland and the United States because it causes allergic and/or intolerance reactions as well as skin sensitivity.
160 (a)	Carotene, alpha-, beta-, gamma-	Orange-yellow colour, converts to vitamin A in the body. No adverse effects are known.
160 (b)	Annatto	Peach colour is a natural dye made from the seed coat of the tropical Annatto tree. There are studies which have found it can cause allergic reactions, headaches and irritability.
160 (c)	Paprika	Red colour made from capsicums. No adverse effects are known.
160 (d)	Lycopene	Red colour taken from tomatoes and pink grapefruit. No adverse effects are known.
160 (e)	Beta-apo-8'-carotenal	Orange colour, no adverse effects are known.
160(f)	Ethyl ester of beta-apo-8'-carotenic acid	Orange colour, no adverse effects are known.
161 (a)	Flavoxanthin	Yellow colour, no adverse effects are known.
161 (b)	Lutein	Yellow/orange colour obtained from marigolds. No adverse effects are known.
161 (c)	Krypto-xanthin	Orange colour obtained from flowers, plants, oranges and egg yolks. No adverse effects are known.
161 (d)	Rubixanthin	Red/orange colour found in rosehips. No adverse effects are known.
161 (e)	Violoxanthin	Orange colour found in plants including pansies. No adverse effects are known.
161 (f)	Rhodo-xanthin	Purple colour found in some plants. No adverse effects are known.
162	Beet red	Purple colour obtained from beetroots. No adverse effects are known
163	Anthocyanins	Red, blue or purple colour obtained from plants. No adverse effects are known.
164	Saffron	Yellow colour, stigma of the crocus flower. No adverse effects are known.
170	Calcium carbonate	White colour, obtained from rocks and shells. No adverse effects are known.

No.	Name	Comments
171	Titanium dioxide	White colour, found in common minerals. No adverse effects are known.
172	Iron oxide	Yellow, red, orange, brown or black in colour. Naturally occurring pigments of iron. Toxic in high doses but no adverse effects are known.
173	Aluminium	Used to give a silvery finish, this used to be banned in New Zealand but is now allowed.
174	Silver	Used for cake decorating, this used to be banned in New Zealand but is now allowed.
175	Gold	Used for cake decorating, this used to be banned in New Zealand but is now allowed.
181	Tannic acid, tannins	Clarifying agent in alcoholic drinks but also used as a colour. No adverse effects are known.

PRESERVATIVES

No.	Name	Comments
200	Sorbic acid	Naturally occurring but can also be made synthetically. Inhibits yeast growth but not bacteria. Possible skin irritant.
201	Sodium sorbate	Salt of sorbic acid (200). No known adverse effects.
202	Potassium sorbate	Neutralised sorbic acid (200). No known adverse effects.
203	Calcium sorbate	Neutralised sorbic acid (200). No known adverse effects.
210	Benzoic acid	Occurs naturally but can also be made by chemical synthesis. Can cause a rash similar to nettle rash with large quantities also causing gastric irritation. When combined with Tartrazine (102) it provokes a very high hyperactive response in children. Can cause asthma, especially in those dependent on steroid asthma medications, is also reputed to cause neurological disorders and to react with sulphur bisulphite (222).
211	Sodium benzoate	Sodium salt of Benzoic acid — see 210.
212	Potassium benzoate	Potassium salt of Benzoic acid — see 210.

213	Calcium benzoate	Calcium salt of Benzoic acid — see 210.
216	Propyl-paraben	Less toxic than Benzoic acid but still a possible contact allergen. Studies are continuing.
218	Methyl-paraben	Mainly used in jellies and preserves. Non toxic in small amounts but can cause allergic skin reactions.
220	Sulphur dioxides	A gas formed when sulphur burns. May cause allergic reactions in asthmatics, destroys vitamin A and B, typical products are beer, soft drinks, dried fruit, juices, cordials, wine, vinegar, potato products.
221	Sodium sulphite	see 220
222	Sodium bisulsulphite	see 220
223	Sodium metabi-sulphite	see 220
224	Potassium metabi-sulphite	see 220
225	Potassium sulphite	see 220
228	Potassium bisulphite	see 220
234	Nisin	Produced by fermentation of substances like milk. No known adverse effects
235	Natamycin	Naturally occurring anti-fungal. Sometimes used medically to treat candidiasis, can cause nausea, vomiting, anorexia, diarrhoea and skin irritation.
249	Potassium nitrite	Not permitted in foods for young children, may cause dizziness, headaches, difficult breathing, possible carcinogen, typical products are meat.
250	Sodium nitrite	Used to inhibit the growth of the bacteria which causes botulism, as a colour fixative, but there is concern that it reacts with stomach acid to form carcinogenic N-nitroso compounds during digestion.
251	Sodium nitrate	see 250
252	Potassium nitrate	see 249
260	Acetic Acid, glacial	This is basically vinegar.

No.	Name	Comments
261	Potassium acetate or potassium diacetate	A diuretic to be avoided by people with reduced kidney function.
262	Sodium acetate	No known adverse effects.
263	Calcium acetate	No known adverse effects.
264	Ammonium acetate	Ammonia salt of acetic acid. Concerns it is a human carcinogen.
270	Lactic acid	Occurs naturally in sour milk. Could cause digestive problems in very young babies.
280	Propionic acid	Occurs naturally in fermented foods. All propionates are thought to be linked with migraine headaches.
281	Sodium propionate	see 280
282	Calcium propionate	see 280
283	Potassium propionate	see 280
290	Carbon dioxide	Used to put the fizz in soft drinks. Safe.
296	Malic acid	Occurs naturally in fruits, mainly used as an acidity regulator or to provide a tart taste. Not recommended for infants and young children.
297	Fumaric acid	Occurs naturally in fruits. No known adverse effects.

ANTIOXIDANTS & ACIDITY REGULATORS

No.	Name	Comments
300	Ascorbic acid	Occurs naturally in fruits and is commonly known as vitamin C. No known adverse effects.
301	Sodium ascorbate	Sodium salt of vitamin C, no known adverse effects.
302	Calcium ascorbate	Calcium salt of vitamin C, no know adverse effects.
303	Potassium ascorbate	Potassium salt of vitamin C, no known adverse effects.

304	Ascorbyl palmitate	Fatty acid of ascorbic acid, no known adverse effects.
306, 307, 308, 309	Tocopherols	Natural fat soluble anti-oxidants also known as Vitamin E. No known adverse effects.
310	Propyl gallate	Synthetic anti-oxidant used in fats and oils. May cause skin irritation, gastric upsets and not recommended for children.
311	Octyl gallate	Synthetic anti-oxidant used in fats and oils. May cause stomach problems, hyperactivity and eczema. Not recommended for children.
312	Dodecyl gallate	See 311
315	Erythorbic acid	Synthetic isomer of ascorbic acid, also known as vitamin C. Used as an anti-oxidant. No known adverse effects.
316	Sodium erythorbate	Produced from beetroot and sugarcane. Used as an anti-oxidant. No known adverse effects.
319	Tert-butylhydro-quinone	TBHQ is a synthetic compound used to preserve fats and oils. In very high doses, it is thought to be acutely toxic to lab animals. It is allowed in foods but the Food and Drug Administration in the US restricts its use to 0.02% of the oil or fat content in foods. A dose of 5g is fatal and large doses can cause stomach tumours, nausea and vomiting.
320	Butulated hydroxy-anisole	BHA was banned in Japan after there were reports of cancerous and benign tumours in the fore stomach of rats fed BHA. A US National Institutes of Health report says that BHA is "reasonably anticipated to be a human carcinogen based on evidence of carcinogenicity in experimental animals." However it is thought that the low intake of BHA shows no increased risk of cancer in humans. Not recommended for children.
321	Butylated hydroxy-toluene	Known as BHT this is a synthetic compound known as synthetic vitamin E used as an anti-oxidant. High doses may cause hyperactivity in children and might have mutagenic effects. Not recommended for children.
322	Lecithin	Fatty substance occurs naturally in animal and plant tissues. A natural emulsifier. No known adverse reactions.
325	Sodium lactate	Natural acid produced from milk sugar.

326	Potassium lactate	see 325
327	Calcium lactate	see 325
328	Ammonium lactate	see 325
329	Magnesium lactate	see 325
330	Citric acid	Occurs naturally in citrus fruits. No known adverse effects.
331	Sodium citrates	Salt of citric acid. No known adverse effects
332	Potassium citrates	See 331
333	Calcium citrates	See 331
334	Tartaric acid	Natural acid found in many plants. No known adverse effects in small quantities
335	Sodium tartrates	Salt of tartaric acid. No known adverse effects
336	Potassium tartrates	See 335.
337	Sodium potassium tartrate	See 335.
338	Phosphoric acid	Natural mineral mined in the US. High doses can be a skin irritant.
339	Sodium phosphates	Salt of phosphoric acid. No known adverse effects.
340	Potassium phosphates	See 339.
341	Calcium phosphates	See 339.
342	Ammonium phosphates	Salt of phosphoric acid. Not permitted in EU or UK. New to food standards. No known adverse effects.
343	Magnesium phosphates	See 339.
349	Ammonium malate	Not permitted in EU, UK or US. Salt of malic acid. No known adverse effects.
350	Sodium malates	Salt of malic acid. No known adverse effects.
351	Potassium malate	See 350.

352	Calcium malates	See 350.
353	Metatartaric acid	Natural, related to tartaric acid. Mainly used in wine. No known adverse effects.
354	Calcium tartrate	Natural salt of tartaric acid. No known adverse effects.
355	Adipic acid	Natural organic acid found in beetroot and sugar cane. No known adverse effects.
357	Potassium adipate	Natural salt of adipate acid. No known adverse effects.
359	Ammonium adipate	Natural salt of adipate acid. No known adverse effects.
363	Succinic acid	Natural acid found in most fruits and vegetables. No known adverse effects.
365	Sodium fumarate	Salt of fumaric acid (see 297). No known adverse effects.
366	Potassium fumarate	See 365
367	Calcium fumarate	See 365
368	Ammonium fumarate	See 365
380	Tri-ammonium citrate	Natural salt of citric acid. No known adverse effects.
381	Ferric ammonium citrate	Complex mixture of ammonia, iron and citric acid found in citrus fruits. No known adverse effects.
385	Calcium disodium EDTA	Calcium salt of EDTA produced synthetically. May cause kidney damage and muscle cramps if used in large amounts.

THICKENERS, STABILISERS & EMULSIFIERS

No.	Name	Comments
400	Alginic acid	Natural ingredient extracted from seaweed. No known adverse reactions.
401	Sodium alginate	Salt of alginic acid. No known adverse effects.

402	Potassium alginate	See 401
403	Ammonium alginate	See 401
404	Calcium alginate	See 401
405	Propylene glycol alginate	A compound of alginic acid. No known adverse effects.
406	Agar	A gel obtained from red algae. No known adverse effects.
407	Carrageenan	A gel obtained from red seaweeds. Large quantities linked to gastrointestinal ulcers, liver damage and effects on immune system. Not recommended for infants or children.
410	Locust bean gum	Gum extracted from Carob tree seeds. No known adverse effects.
412	Guar gum	Gum extracted from seeds. No known adverse effects.
413	Tragacanth	Gum produced from sap. May cause allergic reactions.
414	Acacia gum or gum Arabic	Gum produced from the Acacia tree. Possible allergen, soothes irritations of mucous membranes
415	Xanthan gum	Fermented glucose and sucrose. No known adverse effects.
416	Karaya gum	Gum obtained from a tree. No known adverse effects.
420	Sorbitol	A sugar alcohol. Excess consumption may have a laxative effect and can cause gas and bloating. Not recommended for young children.
421	Mannitol	Natural carbohydrate alcohol present in mushrooms and seaweed. Excess consumption may have a laxative effect, and can cause gas and bloating. Not recommended for young children and not advised for infant food.
422	Glycerin	Natural carbohydrate alcohol. Excess consumption can cause headaches, nausea or thirst.
431	Poly-oxyethene (40) stearate	Synthetic compound. May cause skin allergies in some people
432	Polysorbate 20	Synthetic compound. Conflicting reports argue that large amounts may or may not cause flatulence, diarrhoea and abdominal distension.
433	Polysorbate 80	Synthetic compound. No known adverse effects.
435	Polysorbate 60	Synthetic compound. Some studies show cancerous tumour growth on rats and mice.

436	Polysorbate 65	Synthetic compound. No known adverse effects.
440	Pectins	Naturally occurs in fruit, used as a thickener. No known adverse effects
440 (a)	Pectins	See 440.
440 (b)	Pectins	See 440.
441	Gelatine	Natural thickener extracted from tissue, organs, bones. No known adverse effects.
442	Ammonium phosphatides	Natural carbohydrate alcohol. No known adverse effects.
444	Sucrose acetate isobutyrate	Chemical compound of sucrose. No known adverse effects.
445	Glycerol esters of wood rosins.	Produced from wood rosin. No known adverse effects
450, 451, 452	Diphosphates	Salts of phosphoric acid. No adverse effects known.
460	Powdered cellulose	Prepared from wood and cotton. Not used in baby food in the UK.
461	Methyl-cellulose	Prepared from wood and cotton. No known adverse effects.
463	Hydroxy-propyl-cellulose	Extracted from green plants and algae. No known adverse effects.
464	Hydroxy-propyl-methyl-cellulose	See 463.
465	methy-lethyl-cellulose	See 463.
466	Sodium carboxy-methyl-cellulose	See 463.
470	Salts of fatty acids	Sodium, potassium and calcium salts of fatty acids. Produced mainly from plants. No known adverse effects.
471	Mono- and diglycerides of fatty acids	Produced primarily from hydrogenated soya bean oil. No known adverse effects

472a, 472b, 472c, 472e, 472f	Fatty acid esters of glycerol	Produced from glycerol, natural fatty acids and acetic, lactic, citric, tartaric and diacetyl tartaric acids. No known adverse effects.
473	Sucrose esters of fatty acids	Fatty acids mainly derived from plants. No known adverse effects.
475	Polyglycerol esters of fatty acids	Fatty acids derived from soybean, rapeseed and maize. No known adverse effects.
476	Polyglycerol polyricinoleate	Produced from polyglycerol and castor oil. No known adverse effects.
477	Propylene glycol esters of fatty acids	Fatty acids derived from plants. No known adverse reactions.
480	Dioctyl sodium sulphosuccinate	Produced by reacting octane with maleic acid anhydride then sodium bisulphite. Still being tested for it's effects on children and infants.
481	Sodium lactylate	A sodium salt. No known adverse effects.
482	Calcium stearoyl-2-lactylate	Organic compound produced by combining stearic acid and lactic acid with calcium hydroxide. No known adverse effects.
492	Sorbitan tristearate	may increase the absorption of fat-soluble substances

pH REGULATORS & ANTI-CAKING AGENTS

500	Sodium bicarbonate	Better known as baking soda. No known adverse effects in small quantities.
501	Potassium carbonates	Synthetic compound. No known adverse effects known.
503	Ammonium carbonates	Produced by heating ammonium chloride and chalk. No known adverse effects.
504	Magnesium carbonate	A common antacid and laxative made by exposing magnesium hydroxide to carbon dioxide under pressure. In high concentrations has a laxative effect.

507	Hydrochloric acid	A highly corrosive and strong mineral acid. Stomach and mouth irritant in high doses.
508	Potassium chloride	A natural mineral salt. Large doses may cause gastric ulceration.
509	Calcium chloride	A common salt. No adverse effects known.
510	Ammonium chloride	A natural mineral salt. Should be avoided by people with impaired liver or kidney function.
511	Magnesium chloride	A natural mineral salt. Large doses can act as a laxative.
512	Stannous chloride	Produced by dissolving tin in hydrochloric acid. No known adverse effects.
514	Sodium sulphate	Natural mineral acid. No known adverse effects.
515	Potassium sulphate	Mineral salt. No known adverse effects.
516	Calcium sulphate	Soluble natural compound. No known adverse effects
518	Magnesium sulphate	Commonly known as Epsom salts. Has a laxative effect in high doses.
519	Copper sulphate	Natural mineral salt. No known adverse effects.
526	Calcium hydroxide	Known as pickling lime. No adverse effects in small quantities.
529	Calcium oxide	Known as burnt lime. Safe in small quantities.
530	Magnesium oxide	Known as magnesia. No adverse effects known.
535	Sodium ferrocyanide	Chemical compound. No adverse effects known.
536	Potassium ferrocyanide	Chemical compound. No adverse effects known.
541	Sodium aluminium phosphate	Chemical compound. No adverse effects known.
542	Bone phosphate	Natural compound produced from the residue of bones. No known adverse effects.
551	Silicon dioxide	Commonly known as silica. No known adverse effects when used in food.
552	Calcium silicate	Chemical compound formed by reacting calcium oxide and silica. No known adverse effects.

No.	Name	Comments
553	Magnesium silicates or talc	Synthetic compound produced by hydrating silicate salts of magnesium. Ingredient in talcum powder. Anti-caking agent in table salt. Not to be inhaled.
554	Sodium alumino-silicate	Natural compound. The effect of ingestion of aluminium compounds in humans is unknown.
556	Calcium aluminium silicate	Naturally occurring silicate clay. No known adverse effects.
558	Bentonite	An impure clay prepared from volcanic ash. No known adverse effects.
559	Aluminium silicate (Kaolin)	A clay mineral. No known adverse effects.
560	Potassium silicate	Naturally occurring compound. No known adverse effects.
570	Stearic acid	Natural saturated fatty acid. No known adverse effects
575	Glucono delta-lactone	Natural compound of gluconic acid produced from glucose. No known adverse effects.
577	Potassium gluconate	Natural compound found in fruit, honey, tea and wine. No known adverse effects.
578	Calcium gluconate	See 577.
579	Ferrous gluconate	See 577.
580	Magnesium gluconate	See 577.
586	4-Hexylresorcinol	White powder insoluble in water but soluble in alcohol. No adverse effects known.

FLAVOUR ENHANCERS

No.	Name	Comments
620	L-Glutamic acid	Natural essential amino acid. May cause allergic and hypersensitive reactions, headaches, nausea. Not recommended for use by pregnant women and children.

621	Mono-sodium glutamate (MSG)	Salt of glutamic acid. It is accepted by the NZ Food Standards Authority that some people who consume MSG may experience symptoms such as burning sensations, numbness, chest pain, headache, nausea and asthma but it says that it is okay to have in food as long as it is labelled. They advise people who have symptoms to avoid it where possible.
622	Mono-potassium glutamate	Potassium acid salt of glutamic acid. Similar problems to 621 and 620. Not recommended for use by pregnant women and children.
623	Calcium glutamate	Calcium salt of glutamic acid. Asthmatics and aspirin sensitive people are advised to avoid this.
624	Mono-ammonium L-glutamate	Ammonium salt of glutamic acid. See 623.
625	Magnesium di-L-glutamate	Magnesium acid salt of glutamic acid. See 623.
627	Disodium guanylate	Known as GMP this is the disodium salt of guanylic acid. Should be avoided by asthmatics and not for use in foods for infants and young children.
631	Disodium inosinate	Known as IMP this is the disodium salt of inosinic acid. Should be avoided by asthmatics, gout sufferers, infants and young children.
635	Disodium 5'ribo-nucleotide	Chemical compound. May cause itchy rash and welts in sensitive people. Asthmatics, gout sufferers, infants and children should avoid it.
636	Maltol	Naturally occurring compound found in bark, pine needles and roasted malt. No known adverse effects.
637	Ethyl maltol	Derived from maltol. No known adverse effects.
640	Glycine	Amino acid. No known adverse effects.
641	L-Leucine	Essential amino acid. No known adverse effects.

MISCELLANEOUS

No.	Name	Comments
900	Dimethyl-polysiloxane	Commonly known as silicons. No known adverse effects.
901	Beeswaxes	Beeswax from hives. Can cause allergic reactions in sensitive people.

903	Carnauba wax	Produced for leaves of the Carnauba palm. In cosmetics can cause allergic reactions.
904	Shellac	Natural, organic resin. No known adverse effects.
905b	Petrolatum or Petroleum jelly.	More commonly known as Vaseline. Can inhibit absorption of digestive fats and can have a laxative effect at high doses.
920	L-cysteine and its hydro-chlorides	Naturally occurring sulphur. May interfere with insulin and can react with MSG (621) to cause headache, dizziness.
941	Nitrogen	Inert natural gas. No known adverse effects.
942	Nitrous oxide	Inert gas. Toxic for inhalant abuse.
943a	Butane	Inert natural gas produced from petroleum. No known adverse effect.
943b	Isobutane	Inert natural gas. No known adverse effects
944	Propane	Inert natural gas produced from petroleum. No known adverse effects.
946	Octafluoro-cyclobutane	A refrigerant, propellant and aerating agent. No known adverse effects.
950	Acesulfame potassium	This is a chemical that is 200 times sweeter than sugar. Its approval for use in 1988 was controversial as the Center for Science in the Public Interest, a Washington consumer group, said that animals fed this in two different studies suffered more tumours than others that did not receive the compound. The FDA (Food and Drug Administration) said that four long-term animal studies in dogs, mice and rats had not shown any toxic effects and approved its use.
951	Aspartame	Artificial sweetener known as NutraSweet. Compound prepared from aspartic acid and phenylalanine which is about 200 times sweeter than sugar. There have been objections made that it might cause brain damage and that when used in soft drinks it deteriorates into toxic levels of methyl alcohol under storage conditions. Neither claim was accepted, and it has been approved as a sweetener since 1981. However aspartame must be avoided by people with the genetic condition phenylketonuria or PKU which means a person cannot break down phenylalanine which is an ingredient in aspartame.
952	Cyclamic acid	Artificial sweetener 30 times sweeter than sugar. Not permitted in the US. Studies suggest it is carcinogenic, mutagenic and can cause testicular atrophy in lab animals.

953	Isomalt	Low calorie sweetener derived from beetroot. In high dose can have laxative effect.
954	Saccharin	Saccharin has largely been replaced by aspartame in many foods, because many studies on animals showed that it can cause cancer and increase the potency of other cancer-causing chemicals. In 1977 the American Food and Drug Association asked for it to be banned, but they were unsuccessful. However products containing saccharin were required to have a warning notice printed on their labels. In 1997, the diet-food industry lobbied to get that removed, and in 2000 saccharin was removed from the government list of cancer-causing chemicals and late that year the requirement for a warning notice on labels was lifted.
955	Sucralose	The only non-caloric artificial sweetener made from sugar. No known adverse effects.
956	Aitame	Artificial sweetener 2000 times sweeter than sugar. No known adverse effects.
957	Thaumatin	Natural mix of sweet proteins from the katemfe fruit. No known adverse effects.
961	Neotame	Neotame uses the same two amino acids which make aspartame but it doesn't break down in the body so will not cause reactions that aspartame can. This is a very new sweetener which has only just started appearing in foods.
965	Maltitol and maltitol syrup	Sugar alcohol which comes from maltose. It has 90% the sweetness of sugar but does not contain calories and does not promote tooth decay. It also has a laxative effect if you eat a lot of it. One study of rats found that changes were observed in the adrenal gland, however these were considered to be no cause for concern.
966	Lactitol	Low-calorie sugar free sweetener produced from lactose. Laxative effect in high doses.
967	Xylitol	Natural sugar alcohol found in fruits and veges. Laxative effect in high doses.
968	Erythritol	Low-calorie sweetener which occurs naturally in fruits and fermented foods. Laxative effect in high doses.

ADDITIONAL CHEMICALS

No.	Name	Comments
1100	Amylase	Enzyme which occurs naturally in yeast. No known adverse effects.
1101	Proteases	Enzyme derived from some fruits. No known adverse effects.
1102	Glucose oxidase	Enzyme extracted from fungi. No known adverse effects.
1104	Lipases	Enzyme found in fungi or animal derived. No known adverse effects.
1105	Lysozyme	Enzyme naturally occurs in hen's egg whites also in human tears, saliva, blood and milk. Should be avoided by those allergic to eggs.
1200	Polydextrose	Produced from glucose. Laxative effect in high doses.
1201	Polyvinyl-pyrrolidone	Synthetic additive. No known adverse effects.
1400	Dextrin roasted starch	Natural starch. No known adverse effects.
1401	Acid treated starch	Starch treated with acid. No known adverse effects.
1402	Alkaline treated starch	Starch treated with alkalis. No known adverse effects
1403	Bleached starch	Starch which is bleached to remove impurities. No known adverse effects.
1404	Oxidised starch	Starch oxidised with sodium hypochlorite. No known adverse effects.
1405	Enzyme treated starch	Starch treated with amylase. No known adverse reactions.
1410	Monostarch phosphate	Starch treated with phosphoric acid. No known adverse effects.
1412	Distarch phosphate	Starch prepared with phosphates. No known adverse reactions.
1413	Phosphated distarch phosphate	Starch treated several times with various phosphates. No known adverse effects.
1414	Acetylated distarch phosphate	Starch treated with phosphorus oxychloride and acetic acid. No known adverse effects.

1420	Starch acetate esterified with acetic anhydride	Treated starch. No known adverse effects.
1422	Acetylated distarch adipate	Treated starch. No known adverse effects.
1440	Hydroxy-propyl starch	Treated starch. No known adverse effects.
1442	Hydroxy-propyl distarch phosphate	Treated starch. No known adverse effects.
1450	Starch sodium octenyl-succinate	Treated starch. No known adverse effects.
1505	Triethyl citrate	Compound of citric acid. No known adverse effects.
1518	Triacetin	Compound of glycerol and acetic acid. No known adverse effects.
1520	Propylene glycol	Compound produced from propylene oxide. Large oral doses in animal have caused central nervous system depression and slight kidney changes.
1521	Polyethylene glycol 8000	Organic compound produced by propylene oxide hydration. No known adverse effects.

artificial sweeteners to avoid

These are the four artificial sweeteners I advise you to avoid. All have health concerns attached to them and are on the Center for Science in the Public Interest's list also. See my Food Code Table for more information on each sweetener.

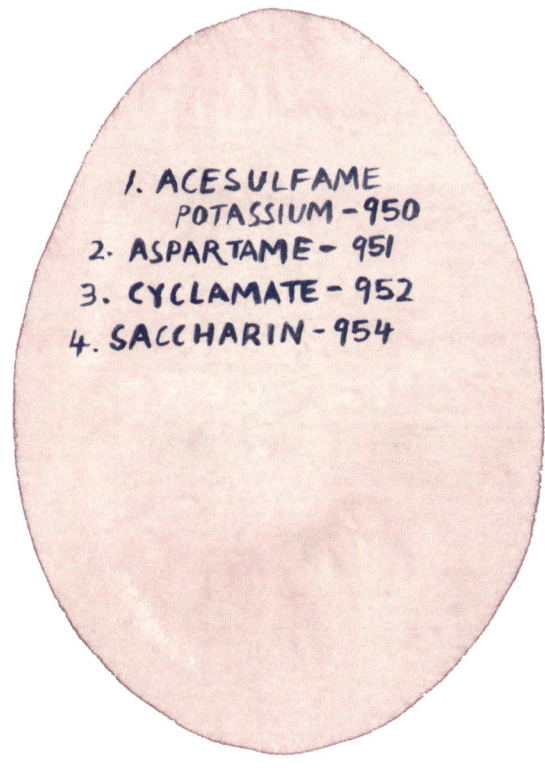

1. ACESULFAME POTASSIUM – 950
2. ASPARTAME – 951
3. CYCLAMATE – 952
4. SACCHARIN – 954

food additives sensitive people should avoid

If you are highly sensitive to food additives and/or suffer from asthma, gout, skin irritations, hyperactivity or bowel looseness then you will want to avoid these additives. See my Food Code Table for more information on each additive.

1. ANNATTO - 160b
2. BENZOIC ACID - 210
3. CAFFEINE
4. CARMINE/COCHINEAL - 120
5. CASEIN
6. GUARANA
7. GUM ARABIC (ACACIA) - 414
8. GUM TRAGACANTH - 413
9. HVP (HYDROLYZED VEGETABLE PROTEIN)
10. LACTOSE
11. MSG (MONOSODIUM GLUTAMATE) - 621
12. QUININE
13. SODIUM BENZOATE - 211
14. SODIUM BISULFITE - 222
15. SULFITES
16. SULFUR DIOXIDE - 220

food additives to avoid

These are the 12 additives I recommend anyone avoid. All have health concerns associated with them and are on the US Center for Science in the Public Interest's list also. See my Food Code Table for more information on each additive.

1. ACESULFAME-POTASSIUM - 950
2. ASPARTAME (NUTRASWEET) - 951
3. BUTYLATED HYDROXYANISOLE (BHA) - 320
4. CARAMEL COLORING - 150a, 150b, 150c, 150d
5. CYCLAMATE (NOT LEGAL IN U.S.)
6. OLESTRA (OLEAN)
7. PARTIALLY HYDROGENATED VEGETABLE OIL (TRANS FAT)
8. POTASSIUM BROMATE - 924
9. PROPYL GALLATE - 310
10. SACCHARIN - 954
11. SODIUM NITRATE - 251
12. SODIUM NITRITE - 250

food colourings to avoid

These are the 14 artificial colourings I think you should avoid. All have health concerns associated with them and many are banned in other countries. See my Food Code Table for more information on each colour.

- 102 Tartrazine
- 104 Quinoline
- 110 Sunset Yellow
- 122 Carmoisine
- 123 Amaranth
- 124 Ponceau 4R
- 127 Erythrosine
- 129 Allura Red
- 132 Indigotine
- 133 Brilliant Blue
- 142 Green S
- 151 Brilliant Black
- 153 Carbon Black
- 155 Brown HT